Communion Thoughts and Prayers

compiled

by Carlton C. Buck

Author of
At the Lord's Table

THE BETHANY PRESS
St. Louis, Missouri

Library of Congress Cataloging in Publication Data

Communion Thoughts and Prayers

Includes indexes
1. Lord's Supper—Prayer-books and devotions—English. 2. Elders (Church officers) I. Buck, Carlton C.
BV826.5.C65   265'.3   76-46943

ISBN: 0-8272-0440-X

Cover by Terri Kurtz

© 1976 by The Bethany Press

All rights reserved. No part of this book may be reproduced by any method without the publisher's written permission. Address: The Bethany Press, Box 179, St. Louis, Mo. 63166.

Scripture quotations, unless otherwise noted, are from the Revised Standard Version of the Bible, copyrighted 1946, 1952, © 1971, 1973 by the Division of Christian Education of the National Council of the Churches of Christ in the U.S.A., and are used by permission.

Manufactured in the United States of America

To all those who faithfully prepare the emblems,
who devotedly preside at the Lord's
Table, and who loyally serve
the loaf and the cup to their
fellow Christians.

Acknowledgments

To the men and women who graciously responded when asked to furnish material for this book, I am deeply indebted.

The following publishers have authorized the use of quoted material: The Bethany Press, St. Louis; Harper & Row, New York; The Boston Music Company, Boston; Abingdon Press, Nashville.

Special acknowledgment is made to the editors of *The Disciple* and its predecessor, *The Christian Evangelist—Front Rank* for the use of poems which were first used in those publications.

To all who helped directly or indirectly, I am grateful. Sherman R. Hanson, Editor of The Bethany Press, gave encouragement and direction; Joye Crespo typed the final draft of the manuscript; my wife, Frieda Helen, made valuable suggestions and shared in the reading of proofs.

Carlton C. Buck

In Sweet Communion

*May the grace of Christ our Saviour,
and the Father's boundless joy,
With the Holy Spirit's favor, rest
upon us from above.
Thus may we abide in union with each
other and the Lord,
And possess in sweet communion joys
which earth cannot afford.*

—*John Newton*

Contents

	Page
Introduction	5
Elders and Their Duties	7
Scriptural Qualifications for Elders	9
Words of Institution	10
Meditations	12
Communion Poems	142
Index of Scripture	150
Index of Topics	153
Index of Authors	155
Index of Poems	156

Introduction

The Lord's Supper belongs to all of Christendom, and the divine invitation to break bread together is for all followers of the One who said, "This is my body . . . do this in remembrance of me." For the Christian Church (Disciples of Christ), the Lord's Table has always had a prominent place in the house of worship and the Lord's Supper a central place in the worship experience. In the Preamble of the Provisional Design, we read, "At the table of the Lord we celebrate with thanksgiving his saving acts and his presence."

Each Lord's Day will find members of our churches gathered about the table in the place of worship, there to "re-enact the divine drama of redemption." And in most of our churches the elders preside at the table offering prayers of thanks and in some instances presenting a communion thought or meditation.

This book, as well as *At the Lord's Table* which preceded it, has been prepared to assist those who serve in this capacity and as a help to anyone who, in self-preparation, would make ready for the weekly appointment with our Lord at his table. The scriptural passages, prayers, meditations, and poems may be used in private devotion as well as in public worship. The Index of Scripture in the back of the book will be helpful in finding material which will harmonize with a certain devotional thought or sermon theme.

In order to provide a variety of presentations for the time of Communion, I asked thirty-five individuals, members of the Christian Church and widely separated geographically, to contribute to the composition of the book. You will find their names under the material they have furnished. Where no name appears under the units, the material has been prepared by me. While the meditations have been written by members of the Christian Church, I do not intend for the material here to be exclusive. The Lord's Supper is for the Church Universal and for all followers of our Lord.

In addition to the sixty general meditations, I have included a suggested service for Maundy Thursday and another for use in homes and hospitals. The prayers, when used in public, need not be used verbatim but should be considered suggestive. The elder may modify, delete, or add to as the occasion may require. In churches where only one prayer of thanksgiving is used, the prayers for the loaf and the cup which appear under the meditations may be combined and used as one.

Many of the meditations in this book have been used in connection with the celebration of the Lord's Supper in the Valley Christian Church of Twin Falls, Idaho. They have been helpful and have proved to be a rich blessing to those assembled about the Lord's Table. It is my sincere prayer that congregations throughout the Brotherhood and beyond may find the book to be helpful and inspirational, and that the experience at the time of the breaking of bread and partaking of the cup may be enhanced because of it. May our Lord, whose Table it is, be ever present as those of us who love him, and who are committed to follow him, break bread together.

Carlton C. Buck

Elders and Their Duties

The elders in the Christian Church (Disciples of Christ) are called to a spiritual leadership in the church. They occupy places of honor and trust among fellow Christians who have chosen them to fill this high office. The office of elder carries with it high standards, and according to the scripture, definite responsibilities. Because of this, some members of the congregation are reluctant to accept the eldership. A feeling of unworthiness may well be a prerequisite for the position. Whoever accepts must be willing to grow spiritually and do the best possible to live up to the high spiritual expectations of the office.

The elders should be resources and consultants in all spiritual matters of the congregation, be available to teach (instruct) where needed according to ability, help guide those who make a commitment for Christ and encourage the deepening of the spiritual life within the congregation. They are to serve at the Lord's Table in turn, be available to take communion to the hospitalized and homebound, help in the conservation of church members, and assist in times of emergency. They are to be supportive to the church board and the various committees, work closely with the worship department, meet with the deacons and deaconesses when necessary to clear signals on the discharge of their duties, and should make recommendations to the church board.

"As the elders help make the Lord's Table meaningful to the congregation, so they can help in elevating the offering to an act of significant worship. First of all, the elder . . . must be a good steward of the things of God. He will sense his responsibility to his heavenly Father and to his fellow Christians who have honored him with a position of spiritual leadership."[1]

The elders will assist the pastor with assigned calling where need may be, attend worship services regularly, even when not serving at the table, support the program of the church in spirit, attitude and conversation, and help in making the offering a responsible act of Christian stewardship. When serving at the Lord's Table, thought should be given to appearance, dress, posture, manner, and attitude. Participation should be one of loving service, joy, and devotion. The elder's mood and attitude will be similar to that of the Psalmist who declared:

I was glad when they said to me,
"Let us go to the house of the Lord!"
—Psalm 122:1

---

1. *At the Lord's Treasury,* by Carlton C. Buck. The Bethany Press, 1959, pp. 16-17. Used by permission.

Scriptural Qualifications for Elders

The saying is sure: If anyone aspires to the office of bishop,[1] he desires a noble task. Now a bishop must be above reproach, married only once, temperate, sensible, dignified, hospitable, an apt teacher, no drunkard, not violent but gentle, not quarrelsome, and no lover of money.

—1 Timothy 3:1-3

For a bishop, as God's steward, must be blameless; he must not be arrogant or quick-tempered or a drunkard or violent or greedy for gain, but hospitable, a lover of goodness, master of himself, upright, holy and self-controlled; he must hold firm to the sure word as taught, so that he may be able to give instruction in sound doctrine and also to confute those who contradict it.

—Titus 1:7-9

---

1. Elder or overseer. See Acts 11:30 and 20:28.

Words of Institution

Now as they were eating, Jesus took bread, and blessed, and broke it, and gave it to the disciples and said, "Take, eat; this is my body." And he took a cup, and when he had given thanks he gave it to them, saying, "Drink of it, all of you; for this is my blood of the covenant, which is poured out for many for the forgiveness of sins. I tell you I shall not drink again of this fruit of the vine until that day when I drink it new with you in my Father's kingdom."

And when they had sung a hymn, they went out to the Mount of Olives.—Matthew 26:26-30.

And as they were eating, he took bread, and blessed, and broke it, and gave it to them, and said, "Take; this is my body." And he took a cup, and when he had given thanks he gave it to them, and they all drank of it. And he said to them, "This is my blood of the covenant, which is poured out for many."—Mark 14:22-24.

And when the hour came, he sat at table, and the apostles with him. And he said to them, "I have earnestly desired to eat this passover with you before I suffer; for I tell you I shall not eat it until it is fulfilled in the kingdom of God." And he took a cup, and when he had given thanks he said, "Take this, and divide it among yourselves; for I tell you that from now on I shall not drink of the fruit of the vine until the kingdom of God comes." And he took bread and when he had given thanks he broke it and gave it to them saying, "This is my body."[1]—Luke 22:14-19.

For I received from the Lord what I also delivered to you, that the Lord Jesus on the night when he was betrayed took bread, and when he had given thanks, he broke it, and said, "This is my body which is broken for you. Do this in remembrance of me." In the same way also the cup, after supper, saying, "This cup is the new covenant in my blood. Do this, as often as you drink it, in remembrance of me." For as often as you eat this bread and drink the cup, you proclaim the Lord's death until he comes.—1 Corinthians 11:23-26. (See also John, chapters 13—17).

---

1. Other ancient authorities add: "which is given for you. Do this in remembrance of me. And likewise the cup after supper, saying, 'This cup which is poured out for you is the new covenant in my blood.' "

Let's Go to Jerusalem

The Text: "As soon as you enter Jerusalem . . ."
—Luke 22:10a (TLB)[1]

Additional Scripture: Luke 22:10b-23.

The Meditation: Yes, let's go to Jerusalem. Let's go to Mt. Zion. Let's climb up the hill, up the tall and steep steps to the upper room, the traditional home of John Mark. To go there is to engage in one of the most solemn, awesome and meaningful experiences one can imagine.

Why so? Because it was in that rock-made structure which has stood like the Master's spirit across the centuries, that Jesus inaugurated a feast of love and remembrance with his close associates, his disciples. In truth, no person visiting there, engaging in quiet meditation, in the singing of "Break Thou the Bread of Life" and in audible prayer, can ever be quite the same. It becomes for the Christian a moment of heart-throbbing devotion and rededication of himself to the Lord of Life whose very physical presence could well have graced that room.

Yet, this is essentially what we do again and again. We do go to the upper room in Jerusalem. We do exactly that each time we gather about the Lord's Table to remember by the breaking of bread and drinking of the fruit of the vine. Whether in some massive cathedral, a wayside church building, or beneath the shading branches of some benevolent tree, we become a part of that enriching experience. And meeting there, we join hands, hearts, and voices with Christlike spirits who share the moment with us from all around the world and all down the centuries.

To go to the upper room is to sit quietly and with the mind's eye see Jesus presiding and to listen to his voice with the soul. "This, my body, broken for you. . . . This, my blood, shed for you . . ."

In our Communion we reconstruct this experience and catch anew the depth of dedication and devotion which characterized his life.

Prayer for the Loaf: As we break this bread together, our Father, may we break from any thought or action that keeps us separated from others and from you. Bind our hearts and lives to the Master, whom to remember is to love as he loved, to serve as he served and to forgive as he forgave. In his name. Amen.

Prayer for the Cup: Dear heavenly Father, in this solemn moment and in this sacred place, we pause to remember the Lord Jesus Christ and his willingness to die upon the cross rather than compromise the cause for which he was sent. And as we partake of this cup, may we just as realistically partake of his life and go from this place to do our full share in the fulfillment of his prayer, "Thy will be done on earth. . . ." In his name. Amen.

J. Clyde Wheeler
Oklahoma City, Oklahoma

---

1. From *The Living Bible* (Wheaton, Illinois: Tyndale House Publishers, 1971) and used by permission.

Entrance into His Presence

The Text: "Come to me, all who labor and are heavy-laden, and I will give you rest."
—Matthew 11:28

Additional Scripture: Matthew 11:25-30.

The Meditation: The Communion stands at the heart of our worship experience, and there is where it should be, for it symbolizes the presence of our Lord. Regular attendance at his Table reinforces our faith . . . not the Table, not even the loaf and cup, but the Christ for whom these stand.

We once had an elder, up in years, whom everyone called "Pop" Greer. When he took his turn at the Lord's Table, and it was time for the meditation and prayer, the congregation was blessed by his love for the Master and his reverence for the Table. Extending his hand until the tips of his fingers touched the Table, he would lean back and pour forth inspiration in words of rare beauty. It was as though, by this action, he made definite contact with heaven. For all assembled, it was a trip into the presence of our divine Lord and refreshment at spiritual springs of living water.

One day I asked him for a copy of one of his meditations. He told me he did not write his words and could not give a meditation unless he was at the Table. He truly seemed to be "turned on" when he reached out and touched the Table.

The Communion should mean this to all of us—an entrance into Christ's presence. It truly gives us an opportunity to express our faith in the living Lord. The cost of our redemption is brought vividly before us and the challenge for the days ahead is made clear.[1]

Prayer for the Loaf: Gracious Lord, we give you thanks for the divine invitation to come into your presence. We hear the word "Come," and we would obey. The world is so much about us, it gives us added joy to come into your presence. As we fellowship together, bless this bread to our spiritual strength, and give us added courage for the tasks ahead. With grateful hearts we partake in the Name above every name. Amen.

Prayer for the Cup: Our heavenly Father, it is our desire to be true followers of Jesus, the Christ. We are grateful for the fruit of the vine which symbolizes his blood shed upon Calvary's cross for the sins of the world. Bless the cup to all who partake this day, and make us more like him who died to save us. This we pray in his name. Amen.

---

1. From *The Christian,* March 26, 1972.

Essential to a Life of Faith

The Text: "Come, buy wine and milk without money and without price. Why do you spend your money for that which is not bread, and your labor for that which does not satisfy?"

—Isaiah 55:1b-2a

Additional Scripture: Isaiah 55:6-13.

The Meditation: Of those common elements of our common life, bread and wine, Jesus said, "This is my body—this is my blood." In that dry and isolated part of the ancient world, there was something almost sacred about bread and wine. In the wilderness, they quarreled for bread which symbolized God's care of them. It was a sin to let a piece lie on the ground and waste. People never tire of bread. It is not a luxury but a necessity—not supplementary but essential.

Yet it has to be personally appropriated, taken and eaten with a sense of need. You can die in sight of it, if you do not take and eat. You must receive it, in the active voice. This is all true of the bread and wine of which Jesus said, "This is my body." It is essential to a life of faith, not supplementary, not a take-or-leave-it affair. It must be received in faith, and its reception is important.

He invites us to dinner, his dinner. Most of us hold a low view of the sacrament, talking about memory, sorrow for his suffering, our unworthiness, etc. But we have said little about taking, eating and drinking *in faith*. This do! Blessed and offered on the one hand, but accepted in faith and consumed on the other hand. Acceptance of the gift means involvement in obedience unto death. Sharing his life means sharing his death. His presence is at the table, but we shall not know it apart from receiving, eating, and drinking in grateful obedience to God. The main part of the event happens when the elements are passed to you.

Prayer for the Loaf: Our heavenly Father, whose mercies are older than our beginnings and who has called us into this fellowship, draw us close to thyself when we extend our frail and earthly hands to take hold of the divine mystery of presence and power. When we eat the bread, grant us health and growth in the family of God. We receive it with thanksgiving and pledge ourselves in obedience unto death in the sharing of Jesus' life. Amen.

Prayer for the Cup: Our God and Father, we hear the call to everyone who thirsts. Food is available without money, and we cannot live without it. When this cup of blessing touches our lips, work a work of grace upon our lives and make it unmistakably your work. May we receive it as that which is essential to the life of faith, even as blood is essential to the body of flesh. When we take the cup, we accept the commission of Christ to be his life and blood in this world. Amen.

J. Daniel Joyce
Houston, Texas

The Re-Creative Work of God

The Text: "For the Son of man came to seek and to save the lost."

—Luke 19:10

Additional Scripture: Luke 19:1-9.

The Meditation: Zacchaeus was a little man, little in every way. He was little in stature and he could not help that, but he was also little in soul. His horizons did not seem to stretch beyond the business of getting money; and he was not overly scrupulous as to how he got it. Then he came into touch with Jesus. That contact with Jesus brought a revolution in Zacchaeus' soul. His wreck of a soul was remade. The spiritual life of Zacchaeus, stunted and starved, was now free to grow. He was in the process of being remade, renewed, fashioned after the pattern of Christ. "Behold I make all things new" (Revelation 21:5).

This re-creative work of God is pin-pointed in this very service of Holy Communion. We come to this table intending to lead a new life. This is not turning over some new leaf. It is a commitment to him who alone can make us anew, as he remade Zacchaeus.

The Holy Communion service bids us look beyond the confines of this lovely sanctuary to a world torn by hatred and near starvation and a large part of its population maimed by poverty and injustice. The Son of Man has come to seek and to save these just as truly as he came to seek and to save those who happen to have been born in a more favored place. Those who are nourished by the Body and Blood of Christ are nourished for service, for the spreading of the light which has illuminated them. The bread and the wine are not luxuries for those who are prepared to loiter by the way. They are warrior's food preparing Christians to go into battle for the Lord.

Prayer for the Loaf: Almighty God, as we receive the bread of life, we realize that in truth we have nothing to offer of our own, for Christ has given us all. We recognize in this loaf a symbol of our freedom from the old bondage and our renewal by the power of the Holy Spirit. Bless to this end, we pray in Jesus' name. Amen.

Prayer for the Cup: Sanctify us, O Lord, as we celebrate the wine of joy. The past is behind us, the future is before us. Enlarge our vision so that we can see the opportunities to serve you and our brothers and sisters. Fill our hearts and dedicate our wills. We ask in Christ's name. Amen.

Samuel W. Hylton
St. Louis, Missouri

A Community of Faith

The Text: For through him we both have access in one Spirit to the Father. So then you are no longer strangers and sojourners, but you are fellow citizens with the saints and members of the household of God, built upon the foundation of the apostles and prophets, Christ Jesus himself being the chief cornerstone.

—Ephesians 2:18-20

Additional Scripture: Ephesians 3:14-20.

The Meditation: One of the things that makes a Communion Service meaningful is the realization that we are thus witnessing to our faith. It says that to be a Christian is more than oneself alone at worship. When we gather together about the table of our Lord, we are part of a group committed to him. We belong to a community of faith. It was his closest disciples that Jesus invited to that upper room for the breaking of bread and prayer.

He said to them, "This do in remembrance of me." He still says it to us as individuals and as members of his church. When we partake of the emblems of his broken body and his shed blood, we do so as part of a great and diverse company of Christians. We who are here today differ from one another in our needs and in our potentialities. Beyond these walls are hosts whom we cannot see. Some are black or brown or yellow of skin. Wherever they dwell, whatever they do, they are part of us. As Paul says, "But now in Christ Jesus you who once were far off have been brought near in the blood of Christ" (Ephesians 2:13). We gather as one body around the Lord's Table.

Prayer for the Loaf: O God, Father of us all, as we gather about this table, enable us to put aside our problems, our fears, our questions. We turn again to you as we seek that inner peace that comes alone from you. May we be ready to listen when you speak to our hearts. We come with personal needs, but also with concern for your people everywhere.

You have taught us to pray, "Give us this day our daily bread." You offer to us now the bread of life. Make us receptive. And at the close of our worship together, send us forth eager to share with our neighbors and fellow-workers, the joy that comes to us because you shared your Son for us. Together in his spirit we now break bread. Amen.

Prayer for the Cup: O Father, we continue to seek your presence in these precious moments here at our Lord's Table. As we drink of this cup, may we be reminded of the supreme price Christ paid on our behalf. As you sent him into the world to redeem us, send us forth to share your message of eternal love. Make us more willing to sacrifice those things which hold us back from complete surrender to you. No one knows what price we may have to pay for our faith but so fill us with your spirit that we may be ready whatever the cost. We drink of this cup now because it represents the Christ to whom we give ourselves anew. In his name. Amen.

Dulcina B. Elliott
Eugene, Oregon

Let Us Celebrate Our New Life

The Text: "I am the good shepherd. The good shepherd lays down his life for the sheep. He who is a hireling and not a shepherd, whose own the sheep are not, sees the wolf coming and leaves the sheep and flees; and the wolf snatches them and scatters them."

—John 10:11-12

Additional Scripture: John 10:1-10.

The Meditation: As disciples of our Lord and Savior, Jesus Christ, let us come together around this table to celebrate our new life in him. Let us gather together to break the bread and to drink of the cup. Let us acknowledge and accept together our common calling to be the people of the God who sent his Son to be as one of us, to show his love for us and to live with us.

In the breaking of this bread, let us confess our sins and ask forgiveness in the name of him who shared with us the experience of humanity, and in obedience to God did not hesitate to present his body in suffering and death in our behalf. As we eat of this bread together let us proclaim by this act that our Lord was indeed—*as us*.

In the drinking from the cup, let us show forth praise to our Lord who loved us so very much that he shed his blood in our behalf. Let us acknowledge that in his laying down of his life as a ransom for us, he became our Paschal Lamb taking away our sins. As we drink together from this cup, we symbolize this act that our Lord was indeed—*for us*.

In celebrating our new life in Christ Jesus in the breaking of the bread and in the drinking from the cup, we do indeed remember the Lord's death until he comes again. By these acts we recall together that God, our Father, has loved us and continues to love us. He demonstrated this by raising our Lord from the dead and seating him at his right hand to intercede for us. We acknowledge that the Paraclete, the Comforter, the Holy Spirit has come to be our counselor and to guide us as we experience the necessities of human existence. As we celebrate with great joy our new life in Christ, we feel his living presence and we know he is ever *with us*.

Prayer for the Loaf: Dear God, our Father, we acknowledge that you loved us so much that you sent your Son to offer his body to the suffering of crucifixion and death for our sins. As we eat this bread, we express our gratitude and our love. In your Son's name. Amen.

Prayer for the Cup: Dear God, our Father, as we drink from this cup, we express our joy and our thanks for our new life in your Son, for we know that by his blood we are saved. In your Son's name, we pray. Amen.

>Walter D. Bingham
>Louisville, Kentucky

Breaking the Loaves With the Hungry

The Text: . . . He looked up to heaven, and blessed, and broke and gave the loaves to the disciples, and the disciples gave them to the crowds.
—Matthew 14:19b

Additional Scripture: Matthew 14:15-20.

The Meditation: Christ set the example for us to follow by being concerned for the needs of people. We remember the compassion he showed when he healed the diseases of people and fed those who were hungry. In the account of the feeding of the five thousand, Jesus disregarded the suggestion of his disciples to send the people away to buy their own food. Instead, he took the loaves and broke the bread for distribution among them.

While the event on that Galilean hillside was one of many fellowship meals, what happened there truly gives us a foretaste of the sacramental character of the Lord's Supper. Bread, which is today called the "staff of life," was used by Jesus to feed the five thousand, and later to represent his body given to his disciples at the Last Supper. Thus, as we eat at the Lord's Table of the living bread of life, we become more aware of our Christian commitments as his body in the world. We can remember that when Christ fed the 5,000, he gave us a message that we should be concerned for the physical as well as the spiritual hunger of people everywhere. For we too can give the bread of life to the thousands by sharing our abundant tables and by truly breaking bread with the hungry.

Prayer for the Loaf: Our gracious heavenly Father, sustainer of life itself and provider of our daily needs, we come to your table aware that our efforts to minister to others are often inadequate. Forgive us when we fail to offer the bread of life to hungry people, whatever their needs may be.

We thank you for this bread, emblem of the broken body of Jesus. May it help us to discern the true meaning of Christ's sacrifice on the cross. May we feed daily on the true bread of heaven until our hearts are filled with love overflowing for others in need, in Jesus' name. Amen.

Prayer for the Cup: Eternal God and Father of us all, you have given us the greatest of all gifts by sending your only Son into the world to bring life everlasting. We ask your forgiveness if we have failed to give a cup of cold water to those in need.

As we partake of this cup, may our eyes be opened to see your way more clearly. And may our hearts be ready to serve you whenever the call is heard. We are thankful to be in the Lord's house around his table to renew our commitments of love and service. Speak to us through this cup that we may go forth to be your witnesses, in Jesus' name. Amen.

> Mary Lou Miller
> Marion, Illinois

Don't Forget Me

The Text: "Do this to remember me."
—1 Corinthians 11:24b (TLB)[1]

Additional Scripture: Luke 4:14-21.

The Meditation: During one of his routine visits to institutional and military chaplaincy centers, Dr. Robert W. Tindall, Director of Chaplaincy Services in the Department of Ministry, Division of Homeland Ministries of the Christian Church (Disciples of Christ), was invited to serve as one of the celebrants at the Lord's Table at an institution for the mentally ill.

The service, proceeding with the usual quiet and dignity accorded the sacrament, was suddenly interrupted from the pew by a patient's cry: "Don't forget me."

There remained stillness and resolute calm; whereupon the patient arose from his seat, approached the chancel of the modest celebration, proceeded behind the table, tapped the acting elder on the shoulder and once again implored: "Don't forget me."

The inhumanities of humankind had left this young man mentally ill, but as the emblems were about to be shared, "deep called unto deep" and he wished to be visited—remembered.

Thirty-three years, by current calculations, are not considered a long time for one to live and three years are not looked upon as a long time to serve. But Christ, our Lord, lived thirty-three years and served three years. Yet, during that time, it is written, "He went about doing good. . . ." "The spirit of the Lord is upon me," He said, "because he has anointed me to preach good news to the poor . . . release to the captives and recovering of sight to the blind . . ." (Luke 4:18).

It's almost sunset now—the future holds for him denial, betrayal, a mock trial and even death on two pieces of wood. Thus, the unforgettable words in his farewell to his disciples for all time and in every clime are still ringing: "Remember me—Do this in remembrance of me." Or did he utter simply, "Don't forget me"?

Prayer for the Loaf: O God, our Father, you have broken the bread of life for the hungering and the thirsting everywhere. Grant to us as we remember you, all that gives life such meaning and purpose as to receive your coveted "well done." In Jesus' name. Amen.

Prayer for the Cup: Our Father, the cup that we take this hour can really be quite empty. Grant that we may so clear our minds and open our hearts that it may be filled with the memory of your sacrificial love, that we may be inspired and challenged to proclaim our faith in you and to participate in the life and work of the whole family of God. In your Son's name, we pray. Amen.

Enoch W. Henry, Jr.
Indianapolis, Indiana

---

1. Taken from *The Living Bible* (Wheaton, Illinois: Tyndale House Publishers, 1971) and used by permission.

We Come as Needy Persons

The Text: Jesus answered her, "If you knew the gift of God, and who it is that is saying to you, 'Give me to drink,' you would have asked him and he would have given you living water."

—John 4:10

Additional Scripture: John 4:7-24.

The Meditation: Jesus was a people person. He loved people, all kinds. Jesus saw past the barriers of race, creed, and sex. The Samaritan woman was not of Jesus' race; her people worshiped on the mountain rather than in a synagogue; and she was a woman, not a man. Any or all of these were enough to keep an ordinary Jewish citizen from even speaking to her.

Jesus did not see an outcast, a foreigner or a second-class citizen. He saw a person needing the living water that he could offer. Today at the Lord's Table, we come as persons free in Jesus Christ. No more deserving than the woman at the well, we come as needy persons asking once again, "Sir, give me this water."

We too are persons caught up in the everyday routine of life. Yet at the Lord's Table all that is common or unworthy in us can be made holy, blessed by this time of fellowship with Jesus. Let us drink of the water of life freely.

Prayer for the Loaf: Our Father who did see good in all people, as we receive this loaf broken for us, may it remind us that your body is broken again when we break relationship with one another. Refresh our spirits, comfort our hearts and forgive us when we forget to be kind. Bless this bread, we pray in the name of him who loved us and gave his life for us. Amen.

Prayer for the Cup: Loving Father, as this cup reminds us that Christ shed his blood that we might become more than we are, let us put aside that which is weak and frail in our lives and be willingly transformed by your love into that which is holy. We realize that it is in us that Christ lives in this world. In his name, we pray. Amen.

>   Sadie Lowrey
>   Boise, Idaho

For the Redemption of Mankind

The Text: For as often as you eat this bread and drink the cup, you proclaim the Lord's death until he comes.

—1 Corinthians 11:26

Additional Scripture: John 17:1-11.

The Meditation: It is a privilege to come around this table and to partake of the sacred emblems. This bread is a symbol of the body of our Lord which he gave to be taken for the redemption of mankind. The cup is a symbol of his blood, given for the remission of our sins. This is the Lord's Table and we come as his guests to share in this experience with him.

In the Disciples' tradition, we come together upon the first day of the week to celebrate his death, burial, and resurrection. The apostle Paul gave us guidance when he wrote:

> For I received from the Lord what I also delivered to you, that the Lord Jesus on the night when he was betrayed took bread, and when he had given thanks, he broke it, and said, "This is my body which is for you. Do this in remembrance of me." In the same way also the cup, after supper, saying, "This cup is

the new covenant in my blood. Do this, as often as you drink it, in remembrance of me." For as often as you eat this bread and drink the cup, you proclaim the Lord's death until he comes.

—1 Corinthians 11:23-26

Prayer for the Loaf: Eternal God, our Father, we thank you for the privilege we have in coming around this, your table, to partake of the bread which is a symbol of your broken body. Grant that we might be worthy of this opportunity. May this bread serve to strengthen our spiritual life. In his name, the name of Jesus Christ our Lord, we pray. Amen.

Prayer for the Cup: Our Father, we come to this, your table, to drink of the cup, not because we feel worthy, but because you have invited us to come. Jesus said that as often as we do this we remember him. Bless this cup and may it give us the spiritual strength to go forth to serve you better. In the name of Jesus Christ, we pray. Amen.

Lorenzo J. Evans
Indianapolis, Indiana

Here Is Offered Renewal

The Text: But far be it from me to glory except in the cross of our Lord Jesus Christ, by which the world has been crucified to me, and I to the world.
—Galatians 6:14

Additional Scripture: Galatians 6:1-10.

The Meditation: We shop and make the godless rich. We vote and give the cynical power. We tune in the TV set and give high ratings to immoral teachings.

The broken body of Christ, symbolized in the loaf, brings forth our deep remorse, surfaces our subconscious guilt, and makes us conscious of our continuing need to repent of our individual acts. These acts separate us from each other, as does our participation in public attitudes which gives false hopes to those who do not serve a true and living God.

Before the Lord, as often as possible, we should die to the lure of lurid advertisement, shun the profits which dehumanize others, and refrain from shoving and pushing to gain power or prestige over those whom Christ challenges us to serve.

The loaf assures that God is tortured with our temptation, empathetic with our fears, and assassinated by our sin so that Christ may administer our redemption. Here is offered renewal, a continuing chance to become dedicated, and an opening for intentional commitment.

Drink from this cup, and yesterday's good intentions will not meet today's challenges. Receive the joy flowing from this reservoir of God's love, and find your hope's sustenance; your mind's reason for standing whole in the midst of divisive secularity. Your body should no longer be burdened by the weight, your mind by the power, or your emotions by the popularity of secular sin.

Christ's blood becomes a force of wholeness strengthening moral courage in a ridiculing crowd, enabling us to reach out in fellowship to each other in order to share redemption in the world, righting wrongs, healing hurts, and binding wounds of broken hearts. The power to share our faith which comforts us is released as God's love nurtures our love and creates new love today, tomorrow, and forever. Hallelujah! Amen! In Jesus' name, Amen!

Prayer for the Loaf: Our Father, sustainer of power, lender of fortunes and sharer of fame, we are grateful for this symbol of the humanity of the crucified Christ.

We come, having given power to those who would pay lip service to your existence, having spent our money with merchants who would corrupt our morality, and seeking the praise of those who ridicule our faith in you.

We pause to identify those sins which are gnawing away in our subconscious minds, filling us with a sense of guilt too painful to admit to any human, but known in the perfect way you shared your Son.

Hear our prayers for the moral courage to make ethical decisions, and to commit only Christian deeds; bring peace to us individually before our private wars ignite a public world conflagration;

help us confess the hoarding of the bread of life, and to share more bread with those who are hungry for food and righteousness.

Allow us to be broken, burdened, and crucified so that we no longer live, until Christ lives more fully in us. In his name we pray. Amen.

Prayer for the Cup: Our Father, eternal hope, everlasting trust and endless love, we shout your praise for this cup of life. You have comforted generations of our families and friends, enabling our lives to be richer and fuller than any people in history.

You have shown us in the lives of humans the power that comes to those able to conquer the intimidation of death, those who fast rather than submit to tyranny, sing hymns in lions' dens, those who were branded heretics in order to free the church from mere institutional survival, dared to ignore creeds and prescribed theoretical doctrines, refused to kill their neighbors because of some superfluous national demand. But most of all, you have shown us the power of those who come to your table to show the world the source of strength of their daily lives, who quietly, humbly and without force, love one another as though love were the law being enforced in all nations.

Praise, glory, and honor to you, God, in the name of Jesus Christ, whose comforter is comforting today as yesterday, and will be there in all the world's tomorrows. Amen.

James L. Blair
Kansas City, Mo.

Communion and Its Underlying Purpose

The Text: Because there is one loaf, we who are many are one body, for we all partake of the same loaf.

—1 Corinthians 10:17

Additional Scripture: 1 Corinthians 10:14-24.

The Meditation: Why did Christ give us the Communion? The ordinance was instituted by him for at least four reasons. One was certainly to perpetuate the fact of the saving work of Christ on Calvary's cross (1 Cor. 11:24). Another reason was to proclaim his death and his return (1 Cor. 11:26). The Communion also identifies the Christian with his Lord. As the Christian partakes of the emblems, he is testifying to the fact of his own personal appropriation of the saving work of Christ. There is still another reason and that is to bring his followers together in the spirit of oneness; a unity one with another (1 Cor. 10:17). Our World Communion each year testifies graphically of this togetherness in him as symbolically Christians around the world sit at the same Table as guests of Christ.

The apostle Paul brings out these reasons basic to the Communion as he writes to the church at Corinth, and we can learn much from this Corinthian passage. We partake "in remembrance" of Christ, but in this remembering, we must do more than recall the scene in the upper room. We must remember who he was, and who he is. We must remember why he died upon the cross, and that he came forth from the tomb and lives among us. We must remember to celebrate his presence and his promise. Communion holds a great deal for us, and we should approach it each Lord's Day in reverence.

Prayer for the Loaf: We realize, our Father, that we do not comprehend all the mystery behind the Communion, but we come in the spirit of humility and worship. As we partake of this loaf, bless it and cause it to bring spiritual health and growth. We express our thanks, seek your forgiveness, and pray for a greater love one for another. This, we pray in Jesus' name. Amen.

Prayer for the Cup: As we partake of this cup, Dear Lord, we are reminded of the words of John the Baptist, "Behold the Lamb of God, who takes away the sin of the world!"[1] We acknowledge that our sin was included and we express our thanks for it. Bless this cup to the nourishment of the spiritual life within us. Make us strong and grant us courage as we face difficult tasks and strength in times of temptation. In the name of Christ, we pray. Amen.

---

1. John 1:29.

His Gracious Invitation

The Text: "I am the bread of life."

—John 6:48

Additional Scripture: Luke 9:18-26.

The Meditation: Jesus Christ is not only the host at the Communion Table. He is also the food. This makes the Communion Table significant in comparison to all other feasts. His gracious invitation is to come and partake of him. The bread which we break is, in itself, not sufficient to satisfy the outward bodily needs, for these are never permanently satisfied. The broken bread, token of his broken body and our broken spirit, our crucifixion; is significant of the satisfaction of an inward hunger, the essential fulfillment of life. The cup which we share was never meant to satisfy a physical thirst, for that kind of thirst is unquenchable. Rather the cup signifies that the essential thirst, which is inward, has been supplied and is being supplied by a living relationship with God in Christ; and in this relationship with one another.

Thus in Communion, Christ not only invites, but he gives himself. He is not only the host, but the food. He not only comes to give bread, he is that bread. He not only offers life, he is that life.

Prayer for the Loaf: O Christ, the bread of life sent from God, invade us anew with your love that we may have an inward appetite for the true bread given by God. Even as you were crucified, help us to put to death within us, all that would hinder us from receiving the food unto life, which is our life, abundant and eternal in you. Amen.

Prayer for the Cup: Lord Jesus Christ, who alone can satisfy our essential and ultimate thirst for life and its meaning and purpose, unite us now with the Father and with you, so that being one with you we may belong to each other in the fellowship of love. By your forgiveness live in us, that the life we live may no longer be our own, but you alive in us now and evermore. Amen.

Vernon Bowers
Pittsburgh, Pennsylvania

The Unseen Host at Every Meal

The Text: ". . . I am with you always, to the close of the age."

—Matthew 28:20b

Additional Scripture: Matthew 28:5-7; 16-20.

The Meditation: There is an old-fashioned motto which still hangs in some homes. It greets the visitor with these words: "Christ is the Head of this home, the unseen Guest at every meal." On many Communion Tables are the words, "Do This in Remembrance of Me." Christ is the "unseen Host" at these Tables on every occasion when the emblems are served.

It is a comfort and a blessing to know that our Lord promised to be with us. This promise followed the giving of "The Great Commission." A few chapters earlier, he had said, "For where two or three are gathered in my name, there am I in the midst of them" (Matt. 18:20). As we come to the Communion Table each Lord's Day, it is well to remember his promise, "I am with you."

As we prepare our hearts and minds for the partaking, let us remember that we come to the Table at the Lord's invitation. We come as guests, yet in a more intimate way, for we are members of his family. He is the Host. We gather at his Table in his name, and he is "in the midst." To a discouraged heart, this can be an oasis in a week of desert-like experiences. Sustenance for the reviving of the spirit is available here. We come because we need to come. We come because we love the One who has issued the divine invitation. We come to satisfy a spiritual hunger; a spiritual thirst. He promised, "I am with you."

Prayer for the Loaf: Our heavenly Father, who has loved us with an everlasting love, we thank you for revealing that love to us through the sacrifice of the Lord, Jesus Christ. We pray for divine forgiveness as we express thanks for the promised Presence of our Lord at this table. Bless the bread which represents his broken body; a body broken for us that we might have life. As we partake of these simple elements, may we be reminded anew of his love, and through them, may we become more like him. This we pray in Christ's name. Amen.

Prayer for the Cup: As we draw near to you, O God, we pray that a genuine sense of your nearness may be our experience. Speak to each heart as we wait before this table, and renew our spirits within us. Again, we express our thanks for the cup which contains the fruit of the vine, and which typifies the shed blood of our Savior. Bless it to our spiritual health, that we may be strong in our service for Christ's church. In his name, we pray. Amen.

A Fresh Revelatory Encounter

The Text: And they devoted themselves to the apostles' teaching and fellowship, to the breaking of bread and the prayers.

—Acts 2:42

Additional Scripture: Acts 2:38-47.

The Meditation: Weekly participation in the Lord's Supper always has been important to me—partly, I am sure, because that is all I have ever known. Disciples founders decided on the basis of their study of the Bible that the supper should be celebrated every Sunday as the central event in a congregation's worship. They read, "On the first day of the week" the church "gathered together to break bread" (Acts 20:7). "Breaking of bread," taken to mean the Lord's Supper, was in a passage that nineteenth-century restorationist Disciples used virtually as an outline of proper worship (Acts 2:42). Whatever legalism there might have been in the original motivation for weekly observance has long since disappeared. I sense that Disciples consider the Lord's Supper indispensable today because it is an effective sign and assurance of the presence of Christ.

On many of our Communion Tables is carved the phrase, "in remembrance of me." We break bread and drink from the cup to remember. Yet "remembrance" as it is prescribed in Paul's account of the institution of the Lord's Supper (1 Cor. 11:23-26) is far more than bringing past events to mind: it is proclamation of the mighty acts of God in Christ, a recalling of the events in history in which God reconciled the world unto himself, a fresh revelatory encounter.

> Kenneth L. Teegarden
> Indianapolis, Indiana

Prayer for the Loaf: Gracious and beneficent God, we come to this table today with great thanksgiving. These symbols awaken our senses to the presence of our Lord who gave himself for us. As we partake of this loaf, help us to put aside all things that would keep us from genuine communion and Christlike fellowship. Bless the bread to our spiritual health, we pray in Jesus' name. Amen.

Prayer for the Cup: Eternal God, giver of good gifts, accept our thanks and bless this cup which brings vividly to our attention the new covenant which was given. Help us to partake in a worthy manner, and to find spiritual reality in the act. Forgive us for any sins of neglect, and grant that we may be strengthened for the divinely-given tasks that are still before us. This we pray in the name of our Lord. Amen.

This meditation is from ***We Call Ourselves Disciples*** *by Kenneth L. Teegarden. Bethany Press, 1975, pp. 86-87. Used by permission.*

Moments of Sacred Fellowship

The Text: For whatever is born of God overcomes the world; and this is the victory that overcomes the world, our faith.

—1 John 5:4

Additional Scripture: 1 John 5:1-12.

The Meditation: Each Lord's Day we enter the moments of sacred fellowship with expectancy, for here at his table we are made aware of his presence in a special and unique way. While the moments may be serious, they should not be somber, and while they may be solemn, they speak of life. We celebrate life, not death; victory, not defeat; joy not sorrow. While we may think of the cross, we remember that Jesus transformed an instrument of torture into a symbol of triumph. "This is the victory that overcomes the world, our faith."

The message that we receive at the Communion Table is one of life. "And this is the testimony, that God gave us eternal life, and this life is in his Son" (1 John 5:11). We are told that those who have the Son have life. The moments of sacred fellowship are moments of rejoicing, moments of thanksgiving, moments of praise. This is true because these moments go beyond mere fellowship with one another and bring us into a meaningful communion with our Maker.

We draw near in reverence, pause, in expectancy, partake to our comfort. These are sacred moments because these emblems represent the very presence of our Lord and the price he paid for our redemption. We come, not because we must but because we may. We come to testify to his goodness and to express our sincere love for him. We come because he bids us come and because we desire to be his true disciples. We break the bread and take the cup in remembrance of Jesus, our Lord.

Prayer for the Loaf: Holy Father of us all, we enter this time of Communion with joy and thanksgiving. In these sacred moments, we draw apart from the work-a-day things of life for a refreshing respite in your presence. We participate in the holy rite, knowing that you are here to bless and that our lives are made stronger by our partaking. As Jesus blessed the loaf in the upper room, bless this bread to us today. This we pray in his name. Amen.

Prayer for the Cup: Gracious and loving God from whom all blessings flow, look upon us this day with mercy for we are aware of our unworthiness. We come, not because we are good but because we want to be better; not because we are strong but because we desire to be stronger. We realize that the cup before us represents the blood shed for our sins. Forgive us Lord, and accept our thanks. Grant us added strength as we face a world in need and endeavor to do the will of him who died for us and lives to companion our souls, even Jesus, the Christ. Amen.

God Reveals Himself

The Text: For it is the God who said, "Let light shine out of darkness," who has shone in our hearts to give the light of the knowledge of the glory of God in the face of Christ." —2 Corinthians 4:6

Additional Scripture: 2 Corinthians 4:1-5.

The Meditation: God reveals himself in various ways. When I first saw a Communion service before I became a Christian, I scoffed at the observance and said within myself, "Do these people think they can make themselves any better just by eating a bite of bread and tasting a sip of juice?"

But now that I have become a Christian I find it does help, and that the face of Jesus Christ does shine most clearly at the Communion Table. Just as we thank God for food in our homes and find his goodness revealed, so at the Communion Table we lift up thanksgiving and find the light of the glory of God in the face of Jesus Christ.

Prayer for the Loaf: Our Father, we come in the name of Jesus who found the deepest holiness in common things. Bless this bread and those who partake that life and sacrifice may stand revealed. We pray in the name of Christ. Amen.

Prayer for the Cup: God of all life and growth, grant us to see within this cup the nature of him who ever shares it with his disciples. As children of his kingdom, may we partake. Amen.

        Frank L. Betzer
        Laramie, Wyoming

A Sacred Appointment

The Text: On Sunday, we gathered for a communion service, with Paul preaching.
—Acts 20:7 (TLB)[1]

Additional Scripture: Luke 22:1-14.

The Meditation: The evidence of the scripture concerning the custom of the New Testament church leads us to believe that they met on the first day of the week and broke bread together. This was done by pre-arranged appointment. Luke tells us, in describing the institution of the Lord's Supper, that "When the hour came" Jesus and the apostles were at the table. This was by appointment. And so it is today when we meet on Sunday morning to break bread together; it is by appointment—a sacred appointment.

Not only do we meet at an appointed time, but at an appointed place. In the first instance, the appointed place was "a large upper room." Perhaps the room was large to suggest the largeness of the fellowship, and today, it's worldwide. Of course, our Lord had a world view when it came to his ministry, and he has passed the challenge of the world outlook on to us. We can also say that the participants at the Lord's Supper are appointed. They are to be friends of Jesus. D. L. Moody once said, "I treat Christ every day as a friend; not as a creed, not as a doctrine."

There is a divinely appointed purpose in our coming to partake of the emblems. We are to do this in remembrance of our Lord. Here, in the practicing of his presence, we are refreshed, renewed, strengthened. We find forgiveness and gain a firmer hold on spiritual reality. Yes, each Lord's Day, we have a sacred appointment.

Prayer for the Loaf: Gracious Lord, we wait humbly before you as we anticipate the receiving of the emblems. By coming here today, we have kept the sacred appointment. May we utilize each moment to the fullest. At this sacred hour, we relive in a dramatic way the scenes of the cross, and we surrender anew to your everlasting love. Bless this loaf for which we lift our thanks, and push back all shadows of doubt. Grant us the joy of your presence now and in the days to come, we pray in the name of Jesus who died for our sins. Amen.

Prayer for the Cup: Eternal God, from whom all blessings come, we realize that this is a time of self-examination, and we pray for your forgiveness. It is also a time of glory and a time of power; so help us to drink deeply of the spiritual springs of living water. Bless the contents of this cup to our need as we partake and as we remember the words of our Lord, "This is my blood of the covenant, which is poured out for many."[2]

---

1. From *The Living Bible* (Wheaton, Illinois: Tyndale House Publishers, 1971) and used by permission.
2. Mark 14:24.

Grace Transforms
Weakness into Power

The Text: "My grace is all you need; power comes to its full strength in weakness."

—2 Corinthians 12:9
(New English Bible)[1]

Additional Scripture: 2 Corinthians 12:7-10.

The Meditation: It is with courage and conviction that we are bold enough to approach the Lord's Table, and to participate with him in remembering his suffering for us in the past, and in anticipating a significant future under the leadership of his ever-present spirit.

Our courage and conviction spring from an acute awareness of our tremendous weakness. The Lord's Table is one of God's great resources for communing with our Creator, receiving new life, meaningful life now, and purposeful power for larger, deeper living in the future.

Someone has said: "When we fail to remember what happened in the upper room, something dies in the life of the church." We gather here today to remember, participate, anticipate, have our weakness transformed into full strength.

We are really here to open our lives wide, wider than ever before in order to make ourselves more available to be immersed in God's resources, receptive to his ever-present spirit, made new in experiencing his grace. We remember because we cannot forget!

Prayer for the Loaf: Our Father, we need your bread—a symbol of grace—the bread of the world shared with us by Jesus Christ, the bread now shared with us through his body, the Church. Thank you for bread which transforms our weakness into power. Amen.

Prayer for the Cup: Our Father, we need your cup—a symbol of grace—the cup of life shared with us by Jesus Christ, the cup now shared with us through the church. Thank you for the cup which enables us to remember, to participate in life now, and to anticipate the continuing leadership of your ever-present spirit. Amen.

James A. Moak
Lexington, Kentucky

---

1. From *The New English Bible,* © The Delegates of the Oxford University Press and The Syndics of the Cambridge University Press, 1970. Reprinted by permission.

Expanding Our Capacities

The Text: "I came that they may have life, and have it abundantly."

—John 10:10b

Additional Scripture: John 10:11-18.

The Meditation: Life at its best is life lived in the will, plan, and purpose of God. Jesus came to make this possible. He gives life abundant. The emblems are placed on the table that we might not forget. We must evaluate Jesus' life by the work he did; his ministry; his life purpose. We must evaluate his death and resurrection by the results they produced. His life sets for us a good example, but his death and resurrection brought to us salvation and the power of a new life.

One time I heard Dr. Raphael H. Miller, in one of his great sermons, say "Our business is not to demand our rights, but to expand our capacities." If anyone follows the Lord Jesus Christ seriously, he will find himself expanding his capacities. The abundant life which our Lord came to give us is ever a growing experience. Regular attendance at his table in communion with him and in fellowship with other Christians gives opportunity for capacity expansion. It nourishes our souls, giving us food for growth.

This and more, we should recognize as we come together about his table. As we partake, we accept the fact of his death and the atonement made possible; we accept the fact of his resurrection and the power of the new life in him. And it is more than a time of memory. Each partaking is a "now" situation. Through it we commune with the living, present Christ. We rejoice as we receive forgiveness, renewal, and a fuller measure of the abundant life. The loaf and the cup are a means to this growing experience.

Prayer for the Loaf: O God, our source of life and love, we come with expectant hearts to this table today. Give us the blessing which best fits our needs and help us to be more like our Master who went about doing good. May the bread which we take be a source of spiritual strength, and may the presence of the living Christ hallow the entire experience. This we pray in his name. Amen.

Prayer for the Cup: For the beauty of holiness, our Father, we give thanks. Our hearts are made glad by the spiritual significance of the Lord's Supper. Bless the cup as we partake and receive our thanks for it. Through our participation, may we find added nourishment for spiritual growth that in turn we may be better able to serve in harmony with your perfect will. In Jesus' name, we pray. Amen.

His Grace at Work in Us

The Text: Whoever, therefore, eats the bread or drinks the cup of the Lord in an unworthy manner will be guilty of profaning the body and blood of the Lord.

—1 Corinthians 11:27

Additional Scripture: 1 Corinthians 11:28-34.

The Meditation: God is at work in us as we partake! Something happens to us as we lift to our lips the Holy Sacrament. We cannot close our minds to those about us; we cannot be unconscious of the fact that there are others sharing. There is one body, and as we partake as one body, we must be conscious of the presence of others.

The eye cannot ignore that the ear is a part of the body also; so we are all a part of one great whole. If we truly interpret the elements of the sacrament to be sacred symbols, we do more than remember his death; we partake with him in death and, as we partake, something happens; God is doing something within us. It is a process of remaking or rebuilding. . . . His grace is at work in us.

The question of unworthiness as stated by the Apostle—is it not present attitude? Is it not what I am thinking now? Is it not what I am allowing God to do with me as I partake? Is his grace present and at work in me, making me something I have not been before? Do I sense anew that I am a part of one body?

God is present in the emblems of sacrifice; symbolic of flesh and blood. He is present in spirit working within us molding these various parts into one great whole. Is it possible that anyone who has acknowledged Christ as the central figure of life can think of this service as anything but sacred? Take . . . eat . . . God is present in you!

Prayer for the Loaf: As we partake, may we sense anew the indwelling presence of your Spirit molding and making us anew. May our lives be a reflection of your grace as we remember the sacrifice of him who gave his life for us. Grant us this awareness, our Father, as we partake of this loaf. Amen.

Prayer for the Cup: As we lift the cup and partake together, O Lord, bless that which is emblematic of his blood. May our lives be transformed by the very presence of his Spirit. Remembering his invitation and promise, this we do in his name. Amen.

Jack Naff
Hermiston, Oregon

Discerning His Body

The Text: For anyone who eats and drinks without discerning the body eats and drinks judgment upon himself.

—1 Corinthians 11:29

Additional Scripture: 1 Corinthians 2:9-16.

The Meditation: Our text refers to a communicant not discerning the body. That is, the person must realize that beyond the emblem is spiritual reality—the Body of Christ represented by the symbol, and that through the partaking, he communes with Christ's spirit. Concerning the bread used in the Communion service, the apostle Paul asked, "Is it not a participation in the body of Christ?" (1 Corinthians 10:16). To us, the partaking is a means of increasing our consciousness of our union with our Lord.

In the additional scripture given above, we find that spiritual things are "spiritually discerned." So, the unspiritual person does not understand nor can he receive rich blessings such a service as the Lord's Supper affords. There is a mystery in the Communion service. It is the mystery of salvation. Why should God love us so much that he would want to send his Son to die upon the cross? Why would the Son love us so much that he would be willing to give himself to save us from sin? We do not know, but it is true and "We love him, because he first loved us" (1 John 4:19. KJV).

So, we come to the Lord's Table with reverence

and great thanksgiving. The sacredness of it demands our undivided attention and prayerful participation. We remember that he said his body was given, broken for us. We remember that beyond the emblems there is the reality of his love and presence.

Prayer for the Loaf: Our Father in Heaven, we thank you for the privilege of being at this service. Help us to "discern the body," and to partake in a worthy manner. May our consecration be complete as we yield to your will, and may our commitment be without qualifications or limitations. As we receive the bread, help us to realize the true significance of it, and bless it to our spiritual enrichment. Hear our prayer, we pray in the name of Jesus. Amen.

Prayer for the Cup: We thank you, our Father, for the cup of communion which brings before us once again the sacrifice of our Savior who poured out his life for us. Forgive us for being less than we should be, and help us to be stronger in our faith and more consistent in our service for you. We recall the Word which tells us that "Greater love has no man than this, that a man lay down his life for his friends."[1] Bless this cup as we partake, and help us to be mindful of its real meaning. This we pray in Jesus' name. Amen.

---

1. John 15:13.

The Word Became Flesh

The Text: The Word became a human being and lived here on earth among us and was full of loving forgiveness and truth.

—John 1:14 (TLB)[1]

Additional Scripture: Ephesians 3:1-12.

The Meditation: The mystery of bread and wine turning into the body and blood of Jesus Christ is not the usual theology of the Christian Church (Disciples of Christ). Although many of us may use the words of institution, quoting Jesus, "This is my body—this is my blood"; yet very few of us feel that the actual transformation takes place. There is a sense of "remembrance" and "celebration," but we may not feel free to talk about the "mystery."

In the same way, we may use the words "The Body of Christ" when we refer to the church or our own congregation, but we have problems dealing with the continuing presence of Jesus Christ as a reality in the midst of our worship service.

Yet a very real mystery is taking place among us when we celebrate the Lord's Supper. A miracle does occur about the Table. The bread and wine (or grape juice many of us use) does become flesh and blood. We who partake are suddenly catapulted into the realm of being the "word becoming flesh." It is perhaps too awesome a responsibility for most of us to accept, but the truth remains; we are part of the Body. We are the *Word* as the Communion elements are absorbed into and become a part of our body. So may the Spirit of Christ become a part of our mind and heart.

Prayer for the Loaf: God, our Father, we give you thanks for this bread for it represents your presence and power. Even as this small bit of material becomes a part of our flesh and permeates our whole body, so may your Spirit enter into our mind and heart to keep and sustain us through this week. In the Spirit of Christ, we pray. Amen.

Prayer for the Cup: Father, as we partake of this cup, we are ever reminded of the sacrifice necessary to sustain and renew your kingdom. We make a new covenant with you today as we pledge ourselves to continue in our discipleship. As the taste of the wine remains in our mouths, so may the remembrance of our vows linger in our minds. Through Christ, our Lord. Amen.

Forrest D. Haggard
Overland Park, Kansas

---

1. From *The Living Bible* (Wheaton, Illinois: Tyndale House Publishers, 1971) and used by permission.

Breaking Bread Together

The Text: Now as they were eating, Jesus took bread, and blessed, and broke it, and gave it to the disciples and said, "Take, eat; this is my body."
—Matthew 26:26

Additional Scripture: Matthew 26:27-30.

The Meditation: The breaking of bread is a universal custom to meet a universal need. Bread is often spoken of as "the staff of life," because it is life-giving. Bread, or food for the body, is a necessity; it is not optional. Jesus, in instituting the Lord's Supper, took something universal, something necessary, something common, something readily available to most people, and used it to symbolize a spiritual truth. He spoke of himself as being "The Living Bread" sent from heaven. He is universal. He is necessary to eternal life. He is available.

In speaking of physical bread, the Scripture tells us that "man does not live by bread alone" (Deuteronomy 8:3). This is because man is more than physical. He is essentially a spiritual being. When we sing, "Let Us Break Bread Together," we are inviting to a life-giving experience. The soul of every human being hungers. That is why we must go beyond the physical to find soul satisfaction. Each person must partake for himself, but in addition to that, each person shares in the wider fellowship. We break bread together. The Lord's Table brings us together. He is central. Our fellowship is in him.

The bread and the cup are simple, everyday things. Jesus made of them a lasting memorial and a perennial blessing. As we gather each Lord's Day to break bread together, we recognize his presence and the life that he gives.

Prayer for the Loaf: Great and loving Father, we have come together to break bread and remember our Savior who gave himself for us. Help us to commune in a way strengthening to us and pleasing to you. And help us to fellowship with one another through the bond of love which binds us to each other and to our Lord. Grant us the grace to share the good things of life with others in all parts of your world. Bless this bread to its intended spiritual use, and our bodies and minds to your service. This we pray in the name of him who died that we might live. Amen.

Prayer for the Cup: It is with joy, O God, that we come to this table. We lift the cup to our lips knowing that the contents symbolize Christ's blood shed for the remission of our sins. Accept our thanks for this and for his holy presence as we obey his command, "Do this in remembrance of me." Forgive our slowness of heart and action in obeying other of his noble commands, and send us forth from here with greater determination to trust and obey. In Jesus' precious name and for his sake, we pray. Amen.

Time to Remember and Obey

The Text: "If you love me, you will keep my commandments."

—John 14:15

Additional Scripture: John 13:31-38.

The Meditation: "A new commandment I give to you," [he said,] " . . . love one another; even as I have loved you" (John 13:34).

And at that moment the meaning of this event rolled off the minds of the disciples like water off a duck's back for they were still angry at having been upstaged by James and John through their mother in the game of "greatmanship."

Only later—after the events of that dreadful night and day—after the unbelievable news that he had risen and those amazing encounters with him—only later when they met together in memory of him did the significance of what he said come through.

He loved in spite of.... he saw and built on their strengths while others sought their weaknesses to cut them down. He counted on a profane and fickle fisherman to be a rock of strength, and Peter became the steady leader of the church in a time of great trial. He saw a person of worth in a woman others condemned as sinner, and Mary became the embodiment of commitment. He stirred a member of the Sanhedrin to come out of the darkness and think in such a new way as to be born again, and it was he who dared to help claim him at the cross.

"A new commandment I give you," he says today, "love one another as I have loved you."

Now it's our time to remember and obey.

Prayer for the Loaf: Our Father, we do know that you love us, but sometimes we forget. Help us, like Jesus, to receive fully your love as we receive this bread and to abide truly in that love. Amen.

Prayer for the Cup: Dear God, as we drink of this cup, open our ears to hear the commandment of your Son, open our whole being to obey. Help us, like him, to seek the strength of those around us so that we, too, may build up the world in our time with love. Amen.

Jean Woolfolk
Indianapolis, Indiana

We Celebrate Our Oneness

The Text: "That they may all be one; even as thou, Father, art in me, and I in thee, that they also may be in us, so that the world may believe that thou hast sent me."

—John 17:21

Additional Scripture: 1 Corinthians 12:1-14.

The Meditation: The Lord's Table brings us together. The very word, "Communion" has "union" in it. Here we are one because we are his. The Table does not belong to the liberal or to the conservative. It does not belong to the ritualistic church or to the informal assembly. It does not belong to the state church nor to the free church. The Table is his. It is at Christ's invitation that we come. It is his sacrifice that brings us together at the Table.

Here at his Table, we are one with the cathedral and the grass-thatched chapel. We are one with the Gothic church and the storefront meeting house. As we partake of the emblems, we become one with his followers around the world no matter what the color or culture may be. As the emblems are taken, some will be kneeling at altars, some will be seated, others will be standing. Some will receive the wafer from the hand of the clergy while others will take the emblem themselves. The words spoken will vary, but inherent in them will be the phrase, "Do this in remembrance of me."

Christ prayed that we "may all be one," and we can help answer his prayer by coming together at his table, and excluding none of his followers from the fellowship. As we break bread together, let us celebrate our oneness.

Prayer for the Loaf: Our loving heavenly Father, so fill us with love that all barriers which separate us from fellow Christians will be broken down, thus opening the way for a oneness of fellowship which will bind us together and with our Lord. Bless this loaf to its intended spiritual use, that our bonds of love may be strengthened. We express our humble thanks for the perfect sacrifice of our Savior in whose name we pray. Amen.

Prayer for the Cup: We are grateful, O God, for the fruit of the vine which symbolizes so beautifully the shed blood of our Lord and Savior. We sense in it "A love poured out and sin forgiven."[1] May the oneness that this Table represents be ours in Christ Jesus in whose name we pray. Amen.

---

1. From "Communion Sonnet," by Carlton C. Buck. Page 177, *At The Lord's Table*, Bethany Press, 1956. Used by permission.

Bread and Wine and Money

The Text: For it is all for your sake, so that as grace extends to more and more people it may increase thanksgiving, to the glory of God.
—2 Corinthians 4:15

Additional Scripture: 1 Chronicles 29:6-14.

The Meditation: Worship expresses in miniature what the church does in life-sized forms in its daily life in the world. This function is illustrated by the offertory. The people of the church bring gifts of money which are collected and taken to the table where they are joined with the bread and wine which have traditionally been the primary offering. This act is done to the singing of words such as "praise God from whom all blessings flow," and is frequently concluded with a prayer in which these physical substances are dedicated to God.

This simple act is fraught with meaning. The elements themselves are radically secular—bread, the product of man's plowing, sowing, waiting, harvesting, milling, baking, selling, buying[1]; wine, fruit of the vine which man cultivates, presses, bottles, and uses, or misuses; money, bits of metal or paper, in themselves of little value, yet the cause of exquisite delight and bitter anguish alike.

Together these elements which he places upon the table symbolize the whole life of man. When he brings them forward, he brings himself as a man of the world who eats and sleeps, who makes love and wages war and plays politics, who rises to nobility at times of self-sacrifice, and who sinks to demonic depths of depravity. All of this he gives to God in the symbols of bread and wine and money.

As he does so, he acknowledges that "all things come of Thee, O Lord, and of Thine own have we given thee.". . .

What these actions mean is that the worshiper offers a sacrifice to God—and he is himself the sacrificial gift. Has not the great Apostle taught him that such self-sacrifice is his acceptable worship of God?

Prayer for the Loaf: Lord and Giver of life, we praise you for bread and all for which it stands—the productivity of the earth that brings forth wheat; the work of many people who harvest, transport, mill, and bake; strength for our work and joy in life.

Most of all we praise you for this bread of the Lord's Supper. With it we offer you our gratitude for the life you give—the life of our common humanity and the new life given us by Jesus. He lived among us, taught your will, suffered and died, rose again, and now makes intercession for us.

As we eat this bread, dear Father, give your Holy Spirit so that the life of Jesus will be renewed in us. And then send us to our work, strong and courageous. Through Christ, our Lord. Amen.

Prayer for the Cup: With this cup of joy, O God, we praise you for Jesus Christ through whom you give us joy and peace, hope and courage, faith and love. We pray that with this cup of salvation you will increase our joy and lead us toward greater maturity in our Christian lives. Drive away our fears and vanities. Counteract our frailties and perversities. And help us to show forth the love of Christ in all we do and say. In his name we pray. Amen.

>   Keith Watkins
>   Indianapolis, Indiana

---

*The meditation is from **The Breaking of Bread** by Keith Watkins, pp. 29-30. Bethany Press, 1966. Used by permission.*

---

1. Ronald E. Osborn, "Bread of the World," *The Pulpit*, XXXV (1964), p. 152.

Our Common Faith

The Text: You are fellow citizens with the saints and members of the household of God.
—Ephesians 2:19b

Additional Scripture: Ephesians 4:1-8.

The Meditation: We have a common faith which binds us together in "the household of God." That faith is in one who made a sacrifice on an altar called a cross. Jesus Christ was both the High Priest making the sacrifice and the sacrifice itself. Our faith in him brings us together in a common bond of fellowship, and as we approach the Communion Table, we celebrate again the sacrifice he made and the victory he won for us.

In verses 4, 5 and 6 in Ephesians 4, the word "one" appears seven times, and each time it is attached to a noun. So we have "one body, one Spirit, one hope, one Lord, one faith, one baptism, one God." These give us the basis for our oneness and an incentive for brotherly love. When we are in communion with Christ at his Table, we are demonstrating our common faith and emphasizing our oneness in him. We must remind ourselves and our fellow Christians of the great truth that the church, which is the body of Christ, is one. And one way to do this is to meet regularly at his Table, and bear witness to the world that we have a common faith in one Lord.

Our contemporary world will be much more impressed by our emphasizing our unity than it will ever be by the propounding of slight differences which may exist. As we break bread together today, let us think on the oneness in our fellowship which is made possible by him for whom these enduring symbols stand. As we do so, we will be remembering him who prayed that all of his followers might be one.

Prayer for the Loaf: O God, our Father, we give thanks for this loaf which represents the broken body of our Lord. We would remember his teachings, his life of service, his death, and his triumphant resurrection. We are here at his invitation and because we love him. Bless this bread as we partake, and draw us closer to our Savior that we may honor him in the way we live. May this rich fellowship in communion with him strengthen our common faith. In the name of Christ, we pray. Amen.

Prayer for the Cup: For this cup, our Father, we give thanks as we remember its significance in relationship to our own redemption. Help us to fix our gaze upon the beauty of him who is "the fairest of ten thousand" to our souls. Forbid that any petty differences should keep us from the glory of oneness in him. In the midst of praise, keep us humble, and in the hardships of life, keep us calm and trusting. This we ask in Jesus' name. Amen.

Love: The First Commandment

The Text: "My Father, if it be possible, let this cup pass from me; nevertheless, not as I will, but as thou wilt."

—Matthew 26:39b

Additional Scripture: Matthew 26:36-46.

The Meditation: Whatever the demand upon the decision-making power in the life of Jesus, he was equal to the occasion. Following baptism, he went into the wilderness where he was confronted with the choice of a life of privilege or a life of ordinary humanity fraught with the hazards of your life and mine. He chose utter humanity. When he saw the consequences of his teaching and healing ministry, he prayed for release but chose the will of the Father. When questioned by Caiaphas and Pontius Pilate he answered in such a way that his doom was sealed. He was crucified!

Jesus was very clear in his own mind about his priorities. The first and greatest commandment is: " 'Hear, O Israel: The Lord our God, the Lord is one; and you shall love the Lord your God with all your heart, and with all your soul, and with all your mind, and with all your strength.' The second is this, 'You shall love your neighbor as yourself.' " (Mark 12:29-31a). His ministry demonstrated this priority unequivocally.

In return for such love on our part, Jesus promised the Father's love, saying, "If a man loves me, he will keep my word, and my Father will love him, and we will come to him and make our home with him" (John 14:23).

Here at his table we are reminded of his death portraying the love of God and his life which was, and is, good news. "Thanks be to God for his inexpressible gift" (2 Cor. 9:15).

Prayer for the Loaf: Gracious God, we thank you for providing the basic needs of our lives. Not the least among these is bread. So often bread is taken for granted. Forgive us. Today we are grateful for its beauty of sun and soil, for the patient labor of those who plant its seed and harvest its fruit; who grind its grain and make its flour; who mold its form and bake its loaves. Even as Jesus blessed bread, his life blesses us in this broken bread. As we partake of it, may it change us into the likeness of Christ. Amen.

Prayer for the Cup: Gracious God, we know that wine was cheap in old Judea. Yet it became the symbol of the blood of Christ and thus immeasurably rich. Throughout our lives we have been prone to cheapen men's blood, seldom hesitating to kill each other in order to survive or get ahead. Forgive us, Lord, for profaning such a rich symbol with our drunken disregard for one another. As this fruit of the vine enters our lives today, may it make our pulses move with the spirit of our Lord and his matchless love. Amen.

Walter F. MacGowan
St. Louis, Missouri

The Preeminence of Christ

The Text: *He is the head of the body, the church; he is the beginning, the firstborn from the dead, that in everything he might be preeminent.*
—Colossians 1:18

Additional Scripture: Colossians 1:9-17.

The Meditation: When we come to the table of Communion, we miss the meaning, the glory and the value unless we partake reverently and prayerfully. This is one time when there should be a complete oneness of soul and a unity of purpose. All minds should be focused upon Christ, the Lord, who must have the preeminence. He is the "head of the body, the church," and members of the body must look to him for guidance. He is the host at the table. He is both the sacrifice and the High Priest. Our love and adoration must be centered upon him.

We come to the house of worship anticipating his presence, and the time of Communion offers us a rich opportunity to breathe the incense of Heaven and to drink deeply from the springs of living water. This experience brings with it the memory of the cross, the promise of eternal life, the relief of forgiveness of sins, and the glory of the divine Presence. Here, we lay aside for a time the cares and toils of everyday living. Here, we draw apart to commune and refresh our souls and minds, and it is here that we find the high moment in our worship experience.

As we hold the bread and cup, let us remember him who first broke it and blessed it to this sacred purpose. And like the great apostle Paul, let us serve, pray and plead that Christ might have the preeminence. Not only in the Communion Service must he be preeminent, but he must be preeminent in or lives, our homes, our businesses.

Prayer for the Loaf: Almighty God, our loving heavenly Father, it is with love and anticipation that we have come to this table and to this moment in our worship service. Bless to each soul here the bread of life for our spiritual nourishment. Forgive our shortcomings, weaknesses, and sins, and strengthen us in the inner person that we may be better able to do your work. We would exalt the Christ in whose name we pray. Amen.

Prayer for the Cup: It is at Christ's command, our Father, that we have come to this Communion Table. His words, "Do this in remembrance of me," resound in our minds and hearts. Bless this cup as we partake that all present may have a greater desire and stronger determination to give Christ the preeminence. Grant us courage to face the tasks yet before us, and the grace to do the will of our Master in whose name we pray. Amen.

The Ultimate Need of Mankind

The Text: For as often as you eat this bread and drink the cup, you proclaim the Lord's death until he comes.

—1 Corinthians 11:26

Additional Scripture: 1 Corinthians 15:20-28.

The Meditation: One of the blessings which has come to mankind out of our technological developments in this century has been the gyrocompass. This instrument, when connected to the navigational mechanism of a ship, takes a position parallel to the axis of the earth's rotation, thus always—in all seasons and in any kind of weather—relates to the geographic North Pole. It holds the course unswervingly, with greater precision than a human helmsman because its "brain" is not subject to fatigue.

The Lord's Supper reminds us that Christ's sacrificial love, expressed supremely by his death on the cross, is to be the unswerving guide for all who claim him as Savior and Lord. Thus, he appointed this Supper to be observed by his followers in remembrance of him.

There are times when we get physically, emotionally, and spiritually fatigued, with a tendency to "get off course." But the cross of Christ has taken a position parallel to the ultimate need of mankind, for it is the way of the Cross which leads to our eternal home.

Prayer for the Loaf: Our heavenly Father, we thank you for your goodness and for your faithfulness toward us in all times, in all seasons. Bless this time we now have, as we break bread together, remembering the broken body of your Son and our Lord and Savior on the cross. Help us to see again the real possibilities for our lives, as we would be guided by your love made known to us through the life, death, and resurrection of Jesus Christ in whose name we pray. Amen.

Prayer for the Cup: We thank you, our heavenly Father, for the direction our lives find in Jesus Christ. As this cup symbolizes the sacrifice of Jesus for our salvation, may our drinking of it now express our commitment to him daily, following the direction of his love and service to all persons. May we be strengthened in our commitment to follow in Christ's way. In Jesus' name we pray. Amen.

> J. Sydney Carnes
> Dallas, Texas

The Meal of Memory

The Text: Remember Jesus Christ, risen from the dead, descended from David, as preached in my gospel.

—2 Timothy 2:8

Additional Scripture: 2 Timothy 2:9-19.

The Meditation: Every time we come to the Communion Table it is a reminder, for on that Table is the meal of memory. It brings to our remembrance the cost of our redemption, the suffering of our Savior and his promise to be with us. There are many memorials, both extravagant and simple—Taj Mahal, Lincoln Memorial, a pair of baby shoes. For the Table of Remembrance, Jesus chose simple, everyday things—the bread made from the wheat of the fields and the wine which comes from the wayside vineyards—perfect symbols for his Body and Blood.

The roots of the Lord's Supper are in the Passover. God had given Israel a covenant, and each time the Passover was observed it was in memory of the deliverance from death. In the Lord's Supper we have the memory of a new covenant between Jesus and his people; a redeemed people, and again there is deliverance from death.

As we partake of the Feast of Remembrance, or Meal of Memory, we recall the advice the apostle Paul gave to Timothy, "Remember Jesus Christ, risen from the dead. . . ." So our participation becomes more than an exercise of memory. It is an acknowledgment of the presence of our divine Lord. We must never allow the press of activities, the toil of everyday work, nor the clamor of things to crowd out this memory nor this acknowledgment.

Prayer for the Loaf: Gracious God, today we come remembering the meaning, the purpose, the Person behind the emblems on this Table. Help us to recall the special times of your nearness and deliverance, and help us to forget the unworthy things in our past which should be forgiven and forgotten. As we partake of this bread, we do so in remembrance of our Lord who gave himself for us that we might have life abundant and everlasting. We remember that he went "about doing good," and we would follow in his footsteps of service. Bless the loaf to our spiritual strength and renewal, we ask in the name of Jesus Christ, our Lord. Amen.

Prayer for the Cup: Our Father, we come here to this Table of Remembrance with thanksgiving and humility. We are thankful for the many blessings showered down upon us, and we are humbled by them. We thank you for memory by which we can recall the blessings of the past and the promise you have given for the future. Bless the contents of this cup, the symbol of Christ's shed blood, and help us never to partake unworthily nor thoughtlessly. As we join with others in partaking, may we do so in memory of the One who loved us and gave himself for us, for it is in his name that we pray. Amen.

The Guest Room

The Text: "The Teacher says to you, 'Where is the guest room, where I am to eat the passover with my disciples?'"

—Luke 22:11

Additional Scripture: Revelation 3:20-22.

The Meditation: There are some unfortunate houses in which no guest ever rests beneath the roof, no table is ever spread for guests and no excited voices of children saying, "Guests are coming to our house!"

Those homes suffer great loss because guests revive and enrich us. Each one is different, each has his own tale to tell. Each stimulates and influences us.

Jesus was shown to a guest room when he wanted to eat the passover with his disciples. He still comes to the door of the soul looking for the kind of hospitality that will welcome him into the guest room.

There are spiritual guests that cross the threshold of some homes—Socrates, Shakespeare, Dante. They come in their books and they are welcome. But of all the spiritual guests that "stand at the door and knock," Jesus is not only the best but the most intimate. He wrote no book. He is not distant in the murky past. He is present here in the midst of human life. We do not merely read of him, he speaks to us. We do not merely learn his thoughts, we come to know him.

He has a place in the guest room of our own soul that has no parallel. We may make the room ready, but we soon discover that he becomes the host and we the guests. He serves the bread that if any man shall eat he shall never hunger again, and he provides the drink by which we shall never thirst again.

Prayer for the Loaf: O God, help us to make our lives as guest rooms for you, and to accept this bread as from your gracious hand. Come in and bless us all! We ask it in your own name. Amen.

Prayer for the Cup: O God of peace, be with us as the host in this feast of love. May our souls be hospitable places where your Spirit can come in and be at home. We would accept this cup as from your gracious hand and make a large place for you today. Come into us, O Lord, and bless us all! We ask it in his name. Amen.

Daniel B. Merrick
Peoria, Illinois

A Table Before Me

The Text: Thou preparest a table before me . . . my cup overflows.

—Psalm 23:5

Additional Scripture: Psalm 23:1-6.

The Meditation: Each Sunday as we meet around the Lord's Table for the Communion service, we acknowledge the love which binds all Christian hearts together. The table has its antecedents in the Old Testament. It was at a Passover Feast that the Lord instituted what we observe as the Lord's Supper. One of the best known and most loved scriptures in the Old Testament is the 23rd Psalm. In it, the Psalmist states that the Lord "Prepares a table before me." This was symbolic of the Lord's care for his people. The table speaks of bounty and blessing.

Today in a real and spiritual sense, he "prepares a table" before us. It, too, is symbolic of his care and provision for his people. We dare not take lightly this table before us, because it bespeaks the price paid for man's redemption. The psalmist mentions that the table is spread in the presence of enemies. Regardless of whatever other typological or theological implications may be involved, history confirms that the Table has always been set in the presence of enemies. Even the upper room held a betrayer.

There is a striking resemblance between the teachings of Jesus and the spiritual tone of the 23rd

Psalm. The faith and confidence expressed in it are much like the teachings of the Master. When the psalmist sings, "Thou preparest a table before me," the mind of the present-day disciple moves quickly and easily to an upper room in Jerusalem and then transcending time and space visualizes a twentieth century church service at a high moment of worship. I am glad and thankful that I belong to a church which keeps "a table before me."

Prayer for the Loaf: Gracious and loving heavenly Father, greatly to be praised, we give thanks today for this Table which is symbolic of your love, care, and provision through the generations. As we partake of the bread, help us to remember our Lord blessed thousands by the breaking of bread during his ministry before Calvary, and has blessed millions by his presence at the Table since the Calvary experience. This we pray in Jesus' Name. Amen.

Prayer for the Cup: Eternal God, we thank you for the great heritage which is ours. We are not unmindful of those in other generations who have kept the faith. Help us in our time to witness to your goodness not only at the Table but in everyday living. Bless this cup as we partake and accept our thanks for this table before us and for all for which it stands. May each person here find rich blessing in the glory of your presence. In Jesus' name. Amen.

Called to Be Wholly Present

The Text: Then he said, "Do not come near; put off your shoes from your feet, for the place on which you are standing is holy ground."

—Exodus 3:5

Additional Scripture: Exodus 3:1-4.

The Meditation: The candles are lit. The cross makes its witness. The table is set with bread and wine. The words of institution have been spoken. All of the accoutrements of liturgy and ritual are being cared for . . . but so often it all seems so routine, so unexciting, so empty!

We have shared in the Supper a multitude of times. Many such occasions have had deep significance, but other times we find ourselves simply going through motions patterned by habit. What makes the difference?

The meaning of the Supper does not depend on us; it is established by God through the life, death, and resurrection of Jesus. The presence of the Holy Spirit does not depend on us; the Spirit is always in the midst of God's people. The invitation to share and partake does not depend on us; it is extended by Christ.

What does depend on us is our attitude as we approach the Supper. Ours is the responsibility for openness. Ours is the effort for receptivity. Ours is the willingness to search for mystery in the midst of the commonplace. Ours is the sensitivity to hear symbolically a voice saying, "Put off the shoes from your feet, for the place on which you are standing in holy ground." Ours is the role of consciously preparing body, mind, heart and soul to "touch and handle things unseen."

The invitation has been extended. We are called to be wholly present . . . for this moment is ever filled with the possibility for "divine-human encounter!"

Prayer for the Loaf: Our Father, bread reminds us of the stuff of our everyday living: our work, our preparation of meals, our activities and obligations. Help us to see more in it this day than merely flour and milk. In the meaning of this moment may it hold for us the presence of him who said, "I am the bread of life," and may our everyday living be transformed. Amen.

Prayer for the Cup: Wine, O God, speaks to us of sacrifice and love. Help us just now to sacrifice our pretense and pride that we may receive in this wine the spirit of him who said, "Greater love has no man than this, that a man lay down his life for his friends,"[1] and thus be set free to serve you whose Kingdom knows no end. Amen.

William C. Howland Jr.
Washington, D. C.

---

1. John 15:13.

Love Seeks and Thirsts

The Text: "Blessed are those who hunger and thirst for righteousness, for they shall be satisfied."
—Matthew 5:6

Additional Scripture: Matthew 5:1-12.

The Meditation: The title of this meditation turns our mind easily to the Communion service. The love of Christ seeks us, and we thirst for that which he has to offer. The emblems on the table are the "ready speech" love offers us each Lord's Day. It is not a message in words, but in a revelation of divine love. God's love went far beyond words, and Christ's love for us was dramatized on a cross. That love is brought to mind every time we partake of the emblems of Communion. True, there is no "ready speech," but there is ready manifestation.

Only spiritual fare can satisfy the higher hungers. Jesus said that when we "hunger and thirst for righteousness" we shall find satisfaction; our hunger and thirst shall be satisfied. Righteousness comes after sustained longing. The Lord's Supper gives us opportunity to translate physical emblems into spiritual reality. And we come again and again to his Table to continue to meet this spiritual need; to satisfy this spiritual hunger and thirst.

This thirst is common to humanity. The psalmist said, "As a hart longs for flowing streams, so longs my soul for thee, O God. My soul thirsts for God, for the living God" (Psalm 42:1-2). It is not flashes of feeling that lead us to the answer of our soul's need, but a hunger and thirst after righteousness which bring us to our soul's satisfaction. Love is truly "a seeking and a thirst."

Prayer for the Bread: O God, like the psalmist, we thirst for you, the living God. We know that nothing else can truly satisfy our hearts. We hunger for the bread of life, and we are thankful for this table spread with these emblems which so beautifully typify the Lord Jesus, who is the bread of Life. Bless to our spiritual strength and satisfaction this bread as we partake. In Jesus' name, we pray. Amen.

Prayer for the Cup: Our gracious and loving Father, we thank you for the spiritual thirst you have placed in each heart, and we thank you for him who satisfies that thirst. Bless this cup and our participation that we may attain a greater measure of righteousness. Forgive us for our lack of spiritual thirst at times and give us an increased awareness of our spiritual needs. Help us to appropriate the blessing that you have for us through the means of this Communion. This we ask in the name of Christ, our Lord. Amen.

We Follow Jesus' Admonition

The Text: The cup of blessing which we bless, is it not a participation in the blood of Christ? The bread which we break, is it not a participation in the body of Christ?

—1 Corinthians 10:16

Additional Scripture: 1 Corinthians 10:17-22, 31-33.

The Meditation: The church is the body of Christ, and Christ is the head of this body—the church. And this manifests the relationship of the members to each other. We are bound together in Jesus Christ the head.

If we did not observe this symbolic reminder of God's great gift through his Son, Jesus, and of Jesus' willingness to suffer and shed his blood to redeem us from our sins, the church as a fellowship would soon disappear. But praise God, we do follow the admonition Jesus gave on the night he was betrayed—"Do this in memory of me."

This fellowship meal reminds us regularly that we are bound together as co-laborers, as partners in suffering, as fellow suffering-servants in the service of our Lord. This observance is a time for self-examination, for soul-searching. The Lord's Supper is a challenge for us to repent, to seek God's forgiveness and for us to forgive, and to rededicate ourselves to better living and more faithful service.

We too must ask, "Lord is it I?" for anyone of us is capable of being a Judas. No man ever experienced agonizing suffering more than our Lord Jesus. His love of people and his spotless life did not deserve his horrible death on the cross. And because Jesus went through it himself, he is able to help others who go through disappointment, thanklessness, misunderstanding, and undeserved suffering.

This is a time of remembering, repenting, and rediscovering God's purpose for our lives.

Prayer for the Loaf. O God, our Father, as we break bread together, help us to remember why; and as we are reminded of the oneness which is available for us as members of the body of Christ, also to remember him who is the head of this body, the church. With gratitude in Jesus' name. Amen.

Prayer for the Cup: Our God and our Father, we know that blood is very life itself, and to give blood to save another is sharing life. Sometimes some of us give a little blood to help sustain the life of another. But your Son and our Savior gave his all so that all who believe and trust and serve him might have eternal life. Thank you, Father, and please help us to be even a little worthy. In Jesus' name. Amen.

Rosa Page Welch
Denver, Colorado

So You Shall Remember

The Text: "So you shall remember and do all my commandments, and be holy to your God."
—Numbers 15:40

Additional Scripture: Numbers 15:37-41.

The Meditation: Through the generations, God has given his people aids to remembrance. In Numbers 15:38, God instructed Moses to tell the children of Israel to put a fringe or tassels on the corners of their garments and to put upon each tassel a cord of blue. This was to proceed through the generations. The purpose of this fringe of blue was explicitly stated, "to look upon and remember all the commandments of the Lord, to do them." The wearer belonged to a heavenly kingdom. A visible aid to remembrance helps in our relationship with God lest we forget.

The psalmist cried, "Some *trust* in chariots, and some in horses: but we will remember the name of the LORD our God" (Psalm 20:7 KJV). And the wise Preacher advised, "Remember also your Creator in the days of your youth." (Ecclesiastes 12:1.) And the great apostle Paul pled, "Remember Jesus Christ, risen from the dead" (2 Tim. 2:8). So it was in the great tradition of helping people remember that Jesus instituted the service of Holy Communion. "Do this in remembrance of me," he said (Luke 22:20). His death was efficacious. His resurrection was victorious. We have much to remember.

Our weekly Communion service helps us to remember all that he did for us and is doing today among his people. It should also help us remember our commitment to him; the good confession we made; our baptism, and the vows and promises we have made. He is faithful to his promises, are we?

Prayer for the Loaf: Help us, O God, that we shall always remember the love and sacrifice of our Lord. Forgive us for forgetting at times that we belong to a heavenly kingdom. Accept our thanks for these visible aids to remembrance, and bless this loaf as we participate in this act of remembering. This we pray in the name of him who remembered us, and gave himself for us. Amen.

Prayer for the Cup: Today we thank you, Lord, for memory and for the great blessing it is to us. We are also thankful for the aids to memory which help to keep us from forgetting. The red in the cup ever reminds us of the blood of Christ shed on Calvary's cross. And we know that the suffering was for us. Bless the emblem and the partaking, we pray in his name. Amen.

Carefully and Prayerfully Prepared

The Text: And the disciples did as Jesus directed them, and they prepared the passover.
—Matthew 26:19

Additional Scripture: Mark 14:12-16.

The Meditation: Three times in the above passage we read the same word—prepare. Jesus and the disciples were preparing to step into this fifteen-centuries-long Hebrew tradition, a high and holy feast remembering the deliverance of Israel from the death angel in Egypt, which persuaded Pharaoh to grant them freedom from slavery. This called for preparation.

During this prepared feast, Jesus chose from the table these two elements, bread and wine. God has a redemption plan for man. Here is help to remember that plan. It is in the broken bread and in the cup. What a big thing to remember. "For God so loved the world that he gave his only Son, that whoever believes in him should not perish but have eternal life" (John 3:16).

Should we not therefore come to this Table with great preparation? The promise is even greater. Ours is more than the deliverance from the bondage of an earthly Pharaoh. Ours is the forgiveness of sins, the most important blessing offered to us by our God, the most needed thing as we stand before our God.

As the emblems were prepared, a deaconess may have prayerfully asked, "Who will take this piece and that piece? Who will take this cup and that cup? He who takes this piece of bread, let him know the love of God that sent Jesus Christ, and he who sups from this cup, let him know that Jesus' sacrifice of his life on the cross was necessary for our redemption." This then is to partake in a "worthy manner."

Prayer for the Loaf: Our Father, as we partake of the loaf, we pray with the poet of old, "Could my tears forever flow, Could my zeal no languor know, These for sin could not atone; Thou must save, and Thou alone: In my hand no price I bring; Simply to Thy cross I cling."[1] Amen.

Prayer for the Cup: We would prepare our hearts, O Lord, for the blessing which awaits our partaking. We express our thanks for redemption of which this cup speaks so eloquently. In Jesus' name. Amen.

                        Jasper C. Havens
                        Boise, Idaho

---

1. From "Rock of Ages, Cleft for Me," by Augustus M. Toplady.

Gladness in His Presence

The Text: I was glad when they said to me, "Let us go to the house of the Lord!"

—Psalm 122:1

Additional Scripture: Acts 2:41-47.

The Meditation: The psalmist was glad when he was invited "to the house of the Lord." The early disciples of Christ broke bread with gladness. The time of Communion offers us such an opportunity. We come, not because it is required. We come, not because it is the proper thing to do. We come, not because others beg us to do so. We come because we are glad that our Lord has given the invitation and it is a joy to come into his presence. And this happiness that is revealed here is a reflection of that greater happiness which awaits them who love and serve our wonderful Lord.

We have a weekly appointment with our Lord, and we should prepare for it. Our bodies, our minds, our hearts should be prepared lest we blunder unprepared into the presence of the Holy One. And as we wait in that Presence, let us ask and receive divine forgiveness. Let us approach the table in humility, and partake with thanksgiving.

We must never allow the Communion Service to become a meaningless routine. Each partaking must be a fresh encounter with spiritual reality. The vitality which Christ's presence affords should cause our hearts to rejoice each time we partake. Into his presence we can bring our burdens, our cares, our spiritual needs. It is here that we can exchange our care for peace, our sorrow for joy. Then we can say with the psalmist, "Thou hast put gladness in my heart."[1]

Prayer for the Loaf: We come with gladness, O Lord, and we rejoice in the goodness shown to us in so many ways. These emblems reflect your great love for us, and we are grateful. As we partake of this loaf placed by loving hands upon this consecrated table, may we do so in loving memory of Christ's sacrifice for us. Bless both the emblem and the partaker, that in the participation each person may truly partake of the bread of life. In Christ's name, we pray. Amen.

Prayer for the Cup: Gracious Father, it is with joy that we come to this Table, and we express our deep thanks for all that it means to us. Help us to remember always the agonies of the cross and the victory of the resurrection morning. Forgive us for the times we are discouraged when we should be claiming the overcoming life through the power of Christ. Bless this cup as we partake, and give us renewal of spiritual strength through it. Accept our thanks and hear our prayer in the name of Christ, our Lord. Amen.

---

1. From Psalm 4:7 (KJV).

Man's Rememberer

The Text: And he took bread, and when he had given thanks he broke it and gave it to them, saying, "This is my body which is given for you. Do this in remembrance of me."

—Luke 22:19-20

Additional Scripture: Mark 14:22-26.

The Meditation: The past holds great treasures. What keys unexpectedly unlock the different rooms where the treasure is kept—an old letter, the snatch of a song, the pungent smells of perfume, the symbols of words! A little click of a lock, and suddenly we find ourselves remembering something we had almost forgotten. The past then is no longer the past; it is a part of the now.

Man has been defined "the animal that remembers." We are what we remember. The strange power of memory reminds us of values, tells us who we are, and conveys meaning to life. It is the key to the contemporary identity crisis.

God has chosen "rememberers, for man"— Moses, the Israelite nation, the Bible, the church. The church is the new Israel. It contains vivid, visible reminders to guard against man's forgetfulness; i.e., candles to remind us "He is the light of the world"; the cross to remind us that a life was invested for our salvation; the emblems of the Table to remind us of the life of our Master and the depth of his love for mankind.

John Calvin once wrote, "No man can have God

as father, who has not had the church as his mother." The church, you see, is the reminder of God to man.

Prayer for the Loaf: Father God, at this sacred Table, we thank you for Jesus Christ, the nobility of his character, the beauty of his spirit, the greatness of his mission, and the dedication of his life. We are humbled that he invested his very body for our spiritual welfare. As we partake of the bread, cleanse us of all that is unworthy and make more complete his image in us. Amen.

Prayer for the Cup: O Lord, as we drink reverently the fruit of the vine, make our souls receptive so that in faith it may be to us the living presence of Jesus Christ. As these emblems enter our body and are assimilated into the bloodstream, so may your Holy Spirit of love and sacrifice permeate all of our being and doing, so that the world may know we are friends of Jesus in whose name we pray. Amen.

> James L. Christensen
> Odessa, Texas

An Act of Faith

The Text: I commend you because you remember me in everything and maintain the traditions even as I have delivered them to you.
—1 Corinthians 11:2

Additional Scripture: Hebrews 11:1-5.

The Meditation: The Lord's Supper or Communion Service is not a magical performance, but an act of faith. The apostle Paul commends the church at Corinth for maintaining the traditions, or as the King James Version has it, he advises the Corinthian Church to "keep the ordinances." Further in the same chapter, he sets about to explain the order of the Lord's Supper.

When we partake of the Lord's Supper, we do it in an act of faith. There is faith in the presence of God. We must remember that "God was in Christ reconciling the world to himself" (2 Cor. 5:19). And we have the promise that our Lord will be with us when we meet together in his name. As we meet together, we do so in the faith that God forgives sin. First John 1:7 tells us that "the blood of Jesus his Son cleanses us from all sin." As he forgives us, we are called upon to forgive one another. This faith in his forgiveness reflects a faith in God's love as shown through the sacrifice of Christ, and this sacrifice is symbolized by the elements on the Table.

> Did e'er such love and sorrow meet,
> Or thorns compose so rich a crown?[1]

Our assembling at the Lord's Table also speaks of our faith in corporate worship. We do not partake alone. This fellowship is a large fellowship; it extends around the world. A little girl twirling a globe, found America, stopped the globe, and kissed her country. She then put her arms around the entire globe. This is what God did. He put his arms around the entire world. When we come to his Table, we come as his family. We need him and we need each other.

Prayer for the Loaf: Our Father in Heaven, we express our thanks for the Lord Jesus Christ and for all that he means to us today. We know that it was your love for our world that brought him to us. We come in faith today to partake of this bread which is symbolic of the bread of life. Bless it to our spiritual health and growth. Forgive us for our sins, and strengthen us against the times of temptation. These blessings we ask in Jesus' name. Amen.

Prayer for the Cup: Gracious God, our Father, who loved us and sent your Son to be our Savior, accept our thanks for the cup which contains the fruit of the vine emblematic of Christ's blood shed for our redemption. May the holy presence of our Lord hallow this place as together we remember him. Grant mercy and grace to each person present that we may honor the name of him who loved us and gave himself for us. Amen.

---

1. From, "When I Survey the Wondrous Cross."—Isaac Watts

Bread for the World

The Text: Jesus said to them, "I am the bread of life; he who comes to me shall not hunger, and he who believes in me shall never thirst."

—John 6:35

Additional Scripture: Exodus 16:13-36.

The Meditation: Manna was the principal food eaten by the Israelites during their forty years of wandering in the wilderness with Moses. This manna was provided daily and had to be gathered daily. Leftover manna was spoiled and inedible. However, an exception was made for the seventh day, a sabbath or day of rest. Since no manna was available on the seventh day, a two-day supply had to be gathered on the sixth day.

This segment of the Exodus story underlines a number of important beliefs of the Israelites: their God provided their daily food (bread); each person received the necessary amount for his/her daily sustenance; food was provided by God but had to be gathered by those who wanted to eat; the "laws" established could not be changed by the "rebels" and by the "lazy" members of the community.

The Gospel According to John finds a direct correlation between the manna of the Israelites and Jesus. Jesus is recognized as manna, or bread, from God. Those who believe in Jesus will have no need for additional food because Jesus satisfies their hunger. Although the Gospel uses figurative language, calling Jesus the bread of life, we recognize that this is also a literal truth. We know that as we live with God, as revealed through Jesus, we do have a new and different life which satisfies our deepest hunger. We also recognize that all of God's children everywhere are called to this new life.

Prayer for the Loaf: We thank you, God, that you give us our daily bread. As we are gathered around this table and as we eat this bread, we recognize that because of you and your love for us and for all peoples everywhere, we do have a new life. We thank you.

As we depart from this table we pray that your presence within us and among us will enable us to share this bread with a hungry world. Amen.

Prayer for the Cup: We thank you for this cup, our Father, and for the reminder that we are called to live a new life in Christ. As you gave fresh water to the Israelites wandering in the wilderness, so do you give us refreshment for our spiritual journey. We drink this cup, acknowledging that our life without you is empty, but through Jesus Christ we find new strength to be your children. Amen.

Faye Feltner
Portland, Oregon

Witnessing for Christ Today

The Text: For I am not ashamed of the gospel: it is the power of God for salvation to every one who has faith....

—Romans 1:16

Additional Scripture: Romans 1:17 and Acts 1:8, 2:38-39.

The Meditation: As we come to the Communion Table, we are not only feeding and strengthening our spirits, we are witnessing for Christ. The apostle Paul was a man of strong faith and bold persuasion. He said, "I am not ashamed of the gospel." When we take our places at the Lord's Table on the Lord's Day, we are telling the world that we are not ashamed; we believe. Then strengthened, we are to take that witness out into the world—still unashamed.

Colin Sterne in his great and challenging hymn, wrote:

> "We've a story to tell to the nations
> That shall turn their hearts to the right,
> A story of truth and mercy,
> A story of peace and light."

He went on to say and cause us to sing, "We've a Saviour to show to the nations." As we are not ashamed to meet with other Christians and break bread together, so we must not be ashamed nor afraid to go from the gathered church and take the "message to give to the nations," as well as to our neighbors.

Jesus said, "This is my body . . . my blood." He also said, "You shall be my witnesses." Do we dare partake and then refuse to witness? We come together to be renewed and strengthened, inspired and blessed. We scatter to take his message to a confused, needy society—a lost world.

Prayer for the Loaf: We lift our hearts in praise and thanksgiving, O God, as we pause at this table of blessing. We are ever in need of infilling and refilling that we may have the continued strength to do your will. As we partake of this loaf broken for us, give us a strong determination to witness, thus fulfilling a responsibility placed upon us by our Master. Bless the partaking to that end, we pray in His name. Amen.

Prayer for the Cup: Blessed God, our Father, we are much in need of spiritual bravery because we never want to be ashamed to witness for him who died for us. In the beautiful but mystic way, cause this cup to be the means of our renewal, that in turn we may be bold in our Christian service. We give thanks for the blood which sealed the New Covenant for our everlasting good. Bless the emblematic cup to each participant and to the praise of our Lord. Amen.

Let God Speak to Us

The Text: Enter his gates with thanksgiving, and his courts with praise! Give thanks to him, bless his name!

—Psalm 100:4

Additional Scripture: Psalm 100:1-5.

The Meditation: We come together in worship to let God speak to us. We come that we might commune with God, for we are a part of the body of Christ. If we are here to let God speak to us out of his word, we should incline listening ears to him. There should always be the atmosphere of devotion and reverence as we "Enter his gates with thanksgiving and his courts with praise!"

Even as Jesus found it necessary to cleanse the temple, so it becomes necessary for us at times to cleanse our own temples. Many times we are just as guilty as the money-changers because of our wrong attitudes and actions. We must develop within ourselves a sensitiveness to the message and the spirit of the Christ and come with open minds and hearts when we worship. Even as the disciples of our Lord continued steadfastly in the apostles' doctrine and fellowship in the breaking of bread and prayer,[1] we too will find that the real marks of growth in our church will be likened unto the early church's spiritual nature. It was feeding upon the word of God, communing with God, that united them in fellowship of prayer and service.

Prayer for the Loaf: Dear God, it is with thanksgiving and praise that we gather about your Table this morning to be reminded once again that you died for our sins. As we partake of the bread may it truly be a symbol of your broken body offered for us. Amen.

Prayer for the Cup: From the beginning of time men have offered sacrifices for their sins. With the coming of Christ, the perfect gift was presented on the altar of time that we might be reminded week after week that your blood was shed for us. Thank you, Lord, for saving us through your Son, who has shown us the more perfect way of life when it is truly committed unto you. Amen.

Herbert P. Davis
Independence, Missouri

The Meditation is from **Preaching on New Testament Themes** *by C. E. Lemmon, p. 100. Bethany Press, 1964.*

---

1. Acts 2:42.

I Have Called You Friends

The Text: "No longer do I call you servants, for the servant does not know what his master is doing; but I have called you friends, for all that I have heard from my Father I have made known to you."
—John 15:15

Additional Scripture: John 15:1-17.

The Meditation: In the south of Mexico, the Zoque Indians describe Communion as "the quality of having and being a friend." However, "the Huastec Indians who live in the broad swampy plains and the mountains along the coast of Tampico, Mexico, speak of Communion in still a different way—'our thoughts are one with God.' Here is the secret of real Communion: identity of thought and purpose. To have Communion with God is to have God's thoughts, as revealed by his Son."[1]

As we gather around the Lord's Table it is well to remember that he is our friend. He has called us friends, and he reminds us in verse 14 of our text, "You are my friends if you do what I command you." So obedience is one way we show our friendship with Jesus. When "our thoughts are one with God," we are on the highest level of communion. Jesus has revealed God's thoughts to us, so this kind of Communion is possible.

It should be encouraging to us as we partake of the emblems he so graciously provided to hear his words again, "I have called you friends," and to remember that he made a way for us to think thoughts in harmony with the will of our heavenly Father.

Prayer for the Loaf: For this divine friendship, O God, we are thankful. Help us to remember that this friendship is possible only because of your love and mercy. Bless this loaf as we partake in this bond of friendship made possible through the grace of our Lord, in whose name we pray. Amen.

Prayer for the Cup: We are grateful, our Father, for the blessings of life, and for the simple things which make the good life possible. For this cup which holds the fruit of the vine, we express our gratefulness. Bless it to our spiritual strength and help us to love like Jesus loved. This we pray in his name. Amen.

---

1. From "A Brochure for the Bible's Day 1958," American Bible Society, New York.

Communion: A Blessing in Any Language

The Text: "Go therefore and make disciples of all nations, baptizing them in the name of the Father and of the Son and of the Holy Spirit, teaching them to observe all that I have commanded you; and lo, I am with you always, to the close of the age."

—Matthew 28:19-20

Additional Scripture: Acts 17:22-31.

The Meditation: Truly the Lord's commandment to his disciples is fulfilled in the world today. At this time when sharing the faith has become the "in thing," it is important that the church remember to maintain the Lord's Table as the center for our sharing the faith.

As my congregation observed World Communion Sunday this past year, it really came to me that the Lord's message has traveled far around the world. We shared in a bilingual/bicultural celebration of Communion with our sister church across town. Gathered around the Lord's Table were people of different ages, customs and colors, all sharing in their own way ideas of what coming to the Lord's Table meant to them. The celebration was made more meaningful when we shared old familiar hymns sung in different languages and experienced the beautiful words of the Avery and Marsh song, "We Are the Church Together."

The young shared their youthful and contemporary music, while the aged, the illiterate, the educated, all shared Christ's love as we sang the closing hymn, "In Christ There Is No East or West." Those words seemed to sum it up pretty well.

Since that experience, I have not been able to come to the Lord's Table without the glorious feeling that I come, not alone, but with thousands of my brothers and sisters across this country and around the world who have been "taught" the sharing of his Body and his cleansing Blood.

Prayer for the Loaf: Father, this loaf might be different in each celebration around the world, but as we partake of it we are all brought to the same understanding that it symbolizes Christ's body given for us all. Bless this loaf and accept our thanks in the name of him whose coming made us one. Amen.

Prayer for the Cup: Father, as we partake of this cup with other Christians around the world in remembrance of our Lord, let us not forget that there are still many waiting for us to share your love with them. We ask your blessing and express our thanks in Jesus' name. Amen.

Luis E. Ferrer
Gary, Indiana

The Lord's Supper Is for All People

The Text: "The Pharisee stood and prayed thus with himself, 'God, I thank thee that I am not like other men . . . even like this tax collector.'"
—Luke 18:11

Additional Scripture: Luke 18:9-14.

The Meditation:
"We have the nicest garbage man,
He empties out our garbage can;
He's just as nice as he can be,
He always stops and talks with me.
My mother doesn't like his smell,
But then, she doesn't know him very well."

This anonymous child's verse is a bit embarrassing to many of us adults. How much do we know about our garbage man? Or have you passed him by all these years because of his "smell"? On a recent Worldwide Communion Sunday, this writer queried his congregation to ascertain how many of them knew their garbage man by name. In a quick poll, with the raising of hands, only fourteen out of 340 worshipers could identify him. Only one of that number had ever extended a dinner invitation. Even the pastor didn't know the name of his garbage collector who had come to his church and home for thirteen years.

Obviously, we get used to those of our own kind—those who attend our school, our church, live in our neighborhood, and shop at the corner supermarket. We rarely go beneath and beyond the "smells" of those who are a trifle different—be they black, white, Jew, Catholic, Jehovah Witness, inner-city slum dweller, or that garbage man over there. The Lord's Supper is for all men—a place where we can accept one another and all accept Christ.

Prayer for the Loaf: Father God, make us to remember how Jesus said, "This is my body which is broken for you," all of you—saints and sinners alike, preferably the latter. Let no one here feel excluded from this observance of the Sacred Supper, even those who may be a bit different from me—even that garbage collector. Give us a greater love for all people, even as Christ's love included all. Amen.

Prayer for the Cup: Father God, make us to remember how Jesus said, "This is my blood which is shed for you," all of you—Pharisees and tax collectors alike. As Christian people, may we encompass that philosophy which claims that "the church is not a country club for the saints, but a hospital for sinners." We seek forgiveness for our prejudice and bigotry, and the blessing of your love, grace, and good will among men. Amen.

Raymond Gaylord
Grand Rapids, Michigan

We Belong to God

The Text: You are not your own; you were bought with a price.

—1 Corinthians 6:19b-20

Additional Scripture: 1 Peter 1:13-21.

The Meditation: The Lord's Table furnishes high moments of inspiration. We come as we are, for we belong to God. We are bought with a price as the scripture tells us. We come seeking the higher moment, the flash of inspiration, the renewal of faith. We come seeking God, and "in our search for him, we are found by him." The moments at his Table help us to find a higher estimate of life. Considering the sacrifice made by our Lord on Calvary's cross for us, we must be important to him.

We should always come to the Communion Table with a quest in our hearts; a quest for greater love, a clearer understanding, a richer experience. Partaking of the spiritual food should give us new strength for life's encounters. Christianity is not an escape from life, it is a definite involvement in life itself. Faith takes hold of life and sets about to discover its real meaning. When we are assembled at the Lord's Table, and remember that we are his, we are assisted with life's quests.

It is here at the Lord's Table that we may find forgiveness, discover our selfhood, and realize a new purpose in life. Peter reminds us that the price God paid for us was "the precious blood of Christ."

This should amplify the meaning behind the emblems which have been lovingly placed upon the Table of Remembrance. This should cause us to remember and renew our vows made in former days. This should bring us in love and humility into the presence of the One who died that we might live. We belong to God.

Prayer for the Loaf: Our Father, we acknowledge our utter dependence upon you. Our hearts respond to the great love which purchased our salvation. As we take these emblems from the table and share in the beauty of the service, renew our faith and strengthen our resolves. Bless the broken loaf which typifies our Lord's Body broken for us that our bodies may be used as living sacrifices in his service. With thanksgiving for his great sacrifice for us, we lift our prayer and praise in his name. Amen.

Prayer for the Cup: Most gracious and loving heavenly Father, we express our thanks for these meaningful emblems and for that divine love which forgives and heals. As we partake of this cup, help us to appropriate its blessings unto our own souls. May the glory of your presence hallow each part of this service, and help us to be partakers of your Spirit. We remember that we were purchased redemptively by our Savior, and we pray in his name. Amen.

God Hears Our Silence

The Text: Out of the depths I cry to thee, O LORD!
—Psalm 130:1

Additional Scripture: Psalm 130:2-8.

The Meditation: The psalmist knew the agony of loneliness. In his cry we hear the timeless cry of all humanity lost in the wilderness of wandering. It was a cry of desperation for the psalmist knew that his sin had cast him so deeply into the depths of despair that only the forgiveness and compassion of God could save him. The cry was not so much a prayer of words said out loud as it was a silent groaning from within.

At one time or another, all of us have experienced this inability to express our feelings. Thus as we approach the Lord's Table, it is important that we distinguish between two kinds of silence: the silence of not having anything to say and the silence of not being able to say anything. The second is the silence of the psalmist, the silence of the depths.

It is in this second silence that Christ intervenes. Romans 8:26 tells us that our needs are communicated to God, "Likewise the Spirit helps in our weakness; for we do not know how to pray as we ought, but the Spirit himself intercedes for us with sighs too deep for words."

As Christians, our faith demands that we believe two things: first, that God hears our silence; second, that his gift of grace to us is real. Both of these are made possible through Christ.

Prayer for the Loaf: Eternal Spirit, hearer of all the silence of the universe, we approach the Lord's Table with reverence and awe. As we eat of this bread we realize that Jesus knew what it was to be broken. In his willingness to give of himself, to experience our pain and feel the weight of the groans of our humanity, he becomes the very means through which we now communicate to you. For that sacrifice and gift of self we are eternally thankful. Amen.

Prayer for the Cup: Eternal Spirit, we know that you are present with us even in the depths of our despair. As we drink of this cup we realize that Jesus knew what it was to empty himself for others. Renew our faith, restore our capacity to dream, and remind us of your covenant of love made possible through your Son and our Savior, Jesus Christ. Amen.

Patrick Overton
Boonville, Missouri

The Miracle of Bread

The Text: Jesus then took the loaves, and when he had given thanks, he distributed them to those who were seated.

—John 6:11a

Additional Scripture: John 6:1-14.

The Meditation: Bread itself is something of a miracle. Sowing, reaping, milling, baking, and the end product is a nourishing morsel of palatable food. As we study the accounts in the New Testament, we find that whenever Jesus touched bread there was an added miracle.

In the account given in our text, we find Jesus feeding the five thousand, and the account appears in the other three Gospels as well. It was another of the signs of Jesus' power and identity. The boy who allowed Jesus to have his five barley loaves watched as Jesus multiplied them to feed the multitude. We too can see our talents multiplied when we bring them to Jesus.

After the resurrection, Jesus appeared to the down-hearted disciples as they trudged along the dusty road to Emmaus. They did not know who he was when they invited him to eat with them. The scripture says, "When he was at table with them, he took the bread and blessed, and broke it, and gave it to them. And their eyes were opened and they recognized him" (Luke 24:30-31). They recognized him when he broke the bread. Perhaps they remembered that a few days before his disciples had been with him in an upper room, and there he had broken the bread, saying, "Take, eat, this is my body."

What took place in the upper room was something of a miracle. The way the room was reserved, the revealing of the betrayer, the institution of the Lord's Supper, along with several other events on that evening, would have to be placed in the category of the unusual. Jesus and the miracle of bread—each time we partake, every sensitive soul must and will feel the welling up of waves of thanksgiving. Bread, a symbol of life, and wine, the symbol of the life blood, cause us to thank God for life and for life eternal.

Prayer for the Loaf: For life abundant and eternal, O God, we give thanks. It is your love that brings us here, and your grace that makes possible forgiveness. Forbid that we should partake as a formal exercise of worship; rather may we sense the true significance of the emblems and the act. Bless this loaf which is so miraculous and so symbolic. This we pray in the name of Christ, our Lord. Amen.

Prayer for the Cup: We pause to lift our hearts in thanksgiving, O God, for this cup of blessing. The fruit of the vine is also a miracle of seedtime and harvest, of sunshine and soil. Keep us mindful that life itself is a miracle and that each day is a precious gift of divine love. As we partake of this cup, may we be reminded of the cost of our salvation. Bless it, dear Lord, we pray in Jesus' name. Amen.

The Table of Grace

The Text: For you know the grace of our Lord Jesus Christ, that though he was rich, yet for your sake he became poor, so that by his poverty you might become rich.
—2 Corinthians 8:9

Additional Scripture: 2 Corinthians 8:1-8.

The Meditation: The Lord's Table is a focal point of faith in understanding the loving grace of God for man. We capture some of the varied meanings of Communion in the titles commonly given: "The Table of Remembrance," "The Table of Thanksgiving," "The Table of Sharing." Through all of these, however, is voiced the central proclamation of God's grace, given to man through his Son, Jesus Christ.

One aspect of grace is a feeling of gratitude and thankfulness. Its place is well expressed by Christians at mealtime, and at other special times.

Another more significant meaning is given in the words of the apostle Paul, "For you know the grace of our Lord Jesus Christ, that though he was rich, yet for your sake he became poor...." Jesus is the supreme example of God's love, doing for us what we do not deserve, nor could ever earn for ourselves. Though he was rich, Christ emptied himself, becoming poor for us. He left his dwelling with God, entered into our world to walk among us. With compassion and courage he ministered to us. He taught us how to live. He was faithful to his purpose, even when it led to a cross that should have been ours. He was victorious over death—for us. We don't deserve it, but he did it for us! He said, "This is my body which is for you. Do this in remembrance of me" (1 Cor. 11:24b). For our sake, Jesus became poor that we might become rich. At the "Table of Grace," we share in this loving grace of God given to us in Christ:

> The grace that cares when Life tumbles in—
> The grace that reassures and helps us walk again when we stumble—
> The grace that sustains and endures when sorrow, loneliness and emptiness threaten to overwhelm—
> The grace that gives thanks, rejoicing for life.

Prayer for the Loaf: Through the loaf, O God, we remember again the great gift of your love given us in your Son Jesus Christ. We gather at his table with thankful hearts for your loving grace which changes lives. We are grateful that the love we share from you can also be shared with others. May this Communion with our Lord truly be a Table of Grace for us, transforming our lives. In Christ's name we pray. Amen.

Prayer for the Cup: Our loving heavenly Father, you have given us grace sufficient for all of life. As we partake of this cup of blessing, we share in the blood of Christ, our Lord, and are reminded that we too stand in the shadow of the cross. Help us appreciate this great gift and make it our own as we endeavor to live faithfully as servants of the living Christ. Amen.

Gordon A. Read
Chaplain, U.S. Navy

Meal of Many Themes

The Text: But if we walk in the light, as he is in the light, we have fellowship with one another, and the blood of Jesus his Son cleanses us from all sin.
—1 John 1:7

Additional Scripture: 1 John 1:1-10.

The Meditation: The Lord's Supper is a meal of many themes. It carries the theme of fellowship, and our text tells us that we have this fellowship when we walk in the light. We are told that the early Christians devoted themselves "to the apostles' teaching and fellowship, to the breaking of bread and the prayers" (Acts 2:42). Our text also speaks of the blood of Jesus, and this is symbolized by the wine on the Communion Table. The theme here is sacrifice, and the sacrifice was made for the cleansing of sin which in turn brings us to the theme of forgiveness. Each time we partake, we can claim forgiveness through the blood of Christ.

Remembrance is another theme of this festive meal. When Jesus instituted the Communion Service, he said, "Do this in remembrance of me." We come remembering—his birth, his life, his teachings, his death, his resurrection and his promises. Then, it is certainly a meal of thanksgiving. Can we remember such a life, such a light, such a love without giving thanks? When we remember the passion and the power of the Person, we are brought to a mood of gratitude. The suffering Savior and the Savior's Supper fill our hearts with adoration and praise. Let us rejoice as we break bread together. Let us give thanks to our Lord for his grace and mercy. Let us celebrate the true meaning of this meal of many themes.

Prayer for the Loaf: O God, the Father of our Lord, and our Father, truly wonderful is the matchless grace of Jesus. We have met in his name to break bread in remembrance of his sacrifice for our sins and to fellowship together around his table. Bless this loaf to its intended use and help us to use our minds and bodies to your service. May we go forth from here better able to meet the demands of life. In his name. Amen.

Prayer for the Cup: Gracious Father, as we partake from this cup, we give thanks for its significance and ask your blessing upon it. We would remember Jesus' blood shed for the cleansing of our sins, and we would walk in the light of his love together. Bless the cup to each one who is here today that each life may be enriched by the partaking. This we pray in the name of him who said, "My peace I give to you," even Christ our Lord. Amen.

A New Covenant to God's People

The Text: For I received from the Lord what I also delivered to you, that the Lord Jesus on the night when he was betrayed took bread, and when he had given thanks, he broke it, and said, "This is my body which is for you. Do this in remembrance of me." In the same way also the cup, after supper, saying, "This cup is the new covenant in my blood. Do this, as often as you drink it, in remembrance of me." For as often as you eat this bread and drink the cup, you proclaim the Lord's death until he comes.

—1 Corinthians 11:23-26

Additional Scripture: Hebrews 8:6-13.

The Meditation: Jesus related perfectly and naturally to his disciples. He knew their needs and understood the traditions of the past. So on the night when it was the custom to observe the Passover, Jesus instituted a new custom, a reminder of God's new covenant with his people. Jesus was constantly reading new light and new life into old customs. The Lord's Supper is a new memorial to his life, his death and his resurrection. Jesus offers to God's people new opportunities for service, for spiritual growth, and for the abundant life.

As one has fellowship with Christians in other parts of the world, how thrilling the observance becomes! The Communion each Lord's Day becomes a worldwide observance of God's promise to his people. It is also a reminder that God has the whole world in his hands. As we celebrate, we long for, and reach out into the community and to the whole world that all may come to him in obedience to his command to love one another, and to grow in his grace.

We rejoice that today Christians eat this meal together binding us to him and binding us to one another. As we gather here today, wellsprings of gratitude flow into our hearts because this supper is for you and for me. It is also for our brothers and our sisters throughout the whole world.

Prayer for the Loaf: Lord, Creator of earth, sea, sky and people, we gather at this Table with joy and with great humility to thank you for the privilege of celebrating our freedom in Christ through his sacrifice of love in our behalf.

We thank you for this bread, symbolic of the new opportunities for a new creative life which we have through your Son, Jesus Christ. We ask forgiveness for the times we have been thoughtless or have acted unkindly to our brothers or sisters. Help us to be big enough in mind and spirit to ask forgiveness. And help us to lift our minds and spirits to a world view of true fellowship with your children in the neighborhood where we live, as well as in other parts of the world.

Accept our thanks, for we are privileged to feast at this spiritual table and to break this bread symbolic of our Lord's broken Body. Amen.

Prayer for the Cup: We continue our thanks for this cup, symbolic of your love poured out upon the earth so that all humankind might learn to love and to grow in Christ. We express our thanks for the hands which have so lovingly prepared this cup and this feast. May it consecrate us anew that we may be able to tell the good news of your love to those who have not heard.

We pray for your blessing upon this cup that it may inspire us to tell the good news of your love by the lives that we live. May our lives reflect the spirit of renewal which we experience at this table today in communion with Christ and in fellowship with those who are gathered in his name. And in his name we pray. Amen.

                            Carnella J. Barnes
                            Los Angeles, California

For a Hungry World

The Text: "I am the living bread which came down from heaven; if any one eats of this bread, he will live forever; and the bread which I shall give for the life of the world is my flesh."

—John 6:51

Additional Scripture: John 6:25-33.

The Meditation: Jesus spoke of giving himself as bread "for the life of the world." He knew of world hunger, and he knew that the greatest hunger was for something more than physical bread. He was well aware that people do not live by material bread alone.

We come to the Lord's Table not to satisfy the physical but to renew the spiritual. Joseph Hall put it vividly, "The heart of man, which is too small to make a meal for a kite, can be satisfied with nothing less than the Lord God Almighty!"[1] This truth fits all people, and Christ's mission was to the whole world. He gave himself to satisfy this world hunger. He is truly bread for a hungry world. He was mindful of people's material needs, but he knew there was a greater need beyond the physical. This is the basis of his discourse on the bread of life. According to our Scripture, the people had followed him across the sea to get more bread—food to eat, and in his discourse, he told them that there was a necessary bread in addition to the kind they were after. He is the bread that satisfies the hunger in the human soul.

We need not only to partake of the living bread, we need to share him with a hungry world.

Prayer for the Loaf: Gracious God, we come to you, the source of life and hope, acknowledging the presence of our Savior who is the bread of life. Help us to partake in a way that will strengthen us spiritually and enable us to share the living bread with others. Bless this loaf as in fellowship we partake, and forgive us where we have failed. As we go from this Communion Service, may we go with a sense of Christ's abiding presence. In his name, we pray. Amen.

Prayer for the Cup: As we take the cup, O Lord, we remember the words, "This is my blood . . . which is poured out . . . for the forgiveness of sins." We accept that forgiveness as we partake. Strengthen us through the partaking that we yield not to temptation in the days before us. Bless the cup and each one who partakes as together we remember your sacrifice on Calvary's cross on our behalf. In the name above every name. Amen.

---

1. The Interpreter's Bible. Vol. 8, p. 568. Abingdon Press, 1952, ed. G. A. Buttrick, *et al.* Used by permission.

Look for the Cross and Find the Church

The Text: Then Jesus told his disciples, "If any man would come after me, let him deny himself and take up his cross and follow me."
—Matthew 16:24

Additional Scripture: Matthew 16:13-23.

The Meditation: As we come to the Lord's Table one of the paramount thoughts that enters our minds is the cross. As we reach to break and bless the bread, our minds reflectively center upon the "wondrous attraction." As we lift the cup of blessing, the whole panoramic vision of Golgotha is cast before us—"his agony, his heavy breath, his awful death." At the Table we are caught in the terrible but wonderful paradox of the cross—"cruel but wondrous." We cannot help but recall our Master's words when he said, "If any person would come after me, let that person deny self, take up the cross and follow me."

The cross reminds us of many things and one of the most significant is its revelation of the true nature and essence of the church, the body of Christ. A number of years ago I was serving a congregation that found it necessary to move from a downtown location to a suburban area several miles away. A beautiful new building was constructed with a seventy-one-foot cross which could be seen from a great distance. A number of people inquired about the easiest way to find the church. After several attempts to respond clearly to this request, someone said, "Just look for the cross and you will find the church." How true that is!

Where is the church today? Just find the cross and you will find the church! The question is often asked, "Is the church relevant?" Indeed it is! And the true church can be found where the followers of Christ are taking up their crosses and following him.

Prayer for the Loaf: Dear Lord, we are thankful for the cross and the simplicity of the emblems. Through this bread and what it represents, we are able to see the extent of your love for us and the extent that your love can be manifested even in our own lives if we are open and receptive. Grant us then the courage to take up our crosses and follow you that the Kingdom might come to a needy world today. Amen.

Prayer for the Cup: Dear Loving God, grant that this cup will become a living symbol in our lives. As this cup represents the cup of blessing, grant that our lives might glorify the blessings you bestow upon us. As this cup represents the cup of hope, grant that our lives might be the vessels of hope for a needy world. As this cup represents the cup of commitment, grant that our lives will become daily a firmer commitment to the love of your Son proclaimed in the living and giving of his life. As this cup represents the bearing of a cross, grant that we might love enough also to take up our crosses and follow you. Amen.

Fredrick Ross Evans
Fullerton, California

Broken for You

The Text: "This is my body, which is broken for you . . ."

—1 Corinthians 11:24 (KJV)

Additional Scripture: Isaiah 53:1-6.

The Meditation: In instituting the Communion, our Lord reminded that his body was broken for us. We break bread together to dramatize the fact. It was his sacrifice that made possible our oneness in him. His brokenness produced our oneness. We dare not allow a broken world to break us from his love.

As we live out our faith in personal ways, we must never forget that we are members of a body, and that we have a collective testimony to bear. As we participate in this ordinance, we are saying to the world about us that his Table is important, that the Christian ethic is valid, that faith is the best way of life. As we come to his Table, we demonstrate our oneness in him for we come in a common faith, in a common Lord.

When Jesus said, "Broken for you," he meant just that. At the chancel steps of Canterbury Cathedral, where many pilgrims have knelt, a guide pressed a man's knee to the step saying, "It is a great thing to kneel where faithful pilgrims have knelt." So it is with us at Communion. At the heart of the church is the heart of him who delivers. We can go forth in victory, forgiven and blessed. Many pilgrims before us have found it true. The words, "Broken for you," must be taken individually and corporately.

Prayer for the Loaf: Eternal God, our Father, during this time of Holy Communion hushed and hallowed, we lift our waiting hearts to you. Our presence here is our prayer, our great need is our plea, and our assurance is your faithfulness. We repent of all that has made our lives earthbound, and pray for forgiveness. May the greatness of the Master flood our souls today, and as we break bread together, may his face shine through. We ask your blessing upon the loaf, that through it Christ's gentleness and love may capture our hearts anew. In his name. Amen.

Prayer for the Cup: We remember the words, O God, that Jesus spoke as he lifted the cup; words about his Blood shed for "the remission of sins." We know that forgiveness for our own sins is included in this gracious act. Bless the cup to the spiritual health of each of us, and accept our thanks for mercy shown, sacrifice made, and sins forgiven. This we pray in the name of him whose followers we are. Amen.

This Cup Called Life

The Text: "And if anyone gives so much as a cup of cold water to one of these little ones, because he is a disciple of mine, I tell you this: that man will assuredly not go unrewarded."
—Matthew 10:42 (NEB)[1]

Additional Scripture: Matthew 10:24-33.

The Meditation: The symbol of the Christian Church (Disciples of Christ) is a cup. Each week as his followers, we assemble around a table and there we share the cup together. How appropriate this is for those who share "this cup called life."

A cup is a container. Its purpose is to be filled. So it is with "this cup called life," that we are sent to drink deeply of the life and teachings of him who is known as the source of the waters of Eternal Life. As we drink of those waters, our lives, like the cup, are filled to overflowing.

A cup, filled, is meant to be shared. So it is with "this cup called life." What a privilege it is to share the waters of eternal life, joy, peace, compassion with others; maybe by giving the "cup of cold water" to those in need. But certainly by coming together week after week, sharing this cup with our church family, our lives are strengthened for the coming week.

So we come and we share. We fill our cups, we dare to empty our cups, daring to be filled again.

Prayer for the Loaf: Our Father, remembering him who is the bread of life, we come to share this day. As we eat of this bread, may it be a reminder to us that you have called us to be your kind of people in this kind of world. As we are willing to share this bread together, may we also be just as willing to share our lives and faith with others. In the name of him who makes a difference, we pray. Amen.

Prayer for the Cup: Father, we bring ourselves here this day daring to ask that you fill our lives anew with your love. As we share this cup of renewal, may it give our lives strength to do your kingdom's work. Be with us now as we share this cup. May it allow us to share our cup called life. Amen.

Tom Rousseau
Tullahoma, Tennessee

---

1. From *The New English Bible,* © The Delegates of the Oxford University Press and The Syndics of the Cambridge University Press, 1970. Reprinted by permission.

Proclaiming the Lord's Death

The Text: For as often as you eat this bread and drink the cup, you proclaim the Lord's death until he comes.

—1 Corinthians 11:26

Additional Scripture: 1 Corinthians 1:18-25.

The Meditation: Teaching, preaching, spreading the Good News has been incumbent upon the followers of Christ since the beginning of the early church. The apostle Paul stated forcefully, "We preach Christ crucified" (1 Cor. 1:23). In giving the order and significance of the Lord's Supper, Paul states that in our partaking we "proclaim the Lord's death."

"All Christians were, and are, called to preach. Some preach and teach by word, by voice; all may preach, teach, proclaim by participation in communion. In a very real sense, the observance of communion is the 'common preaching' or universal proclamation of the church. . . .

"What we do wherever and whenever we join in Holy Communion is integral and essential to our Christian way of life: it is, in dramatic form, the witnessing, the preaching, the proclaiming for which all of us are commissioned as disciples of Christ."[1]

The silent witness that we give as we gather together about the Lord's Table and break bread in Christian fellowship is eloquent. By our very presence and action, we are announcing to the world that we believe in the Christ of the cross, in his resurrection and living presence. Our weekly participation is a continuous proclamation of the salient facts of our faith. Here we acknowledge Christ as our Lord and Savior, and here we proclaim the validity of a commitment which calls upon one to follow the teachings of our Lord.

Prayer for the Loaf: As we gather once again, Our Father, to witness to our faith, we ask your divine blessing upon the loaf which is so beautifully emblematic of the Body of our Lord who allowed the brokenness that we might be made whole. Forgive us our sins and cleanse us from all unrighteousness, and accept our thanks in the name of him whose death we proclaim, even Christ, our Lord. Amen.

Prayer for the Cup: Our heavenly Father, great and good, we reach out for the cup in an act of faith, knowing that because of your mercy, love and grace, a blessing awaits us. May the contents of this cup, symbolic of the shed blood of Christ, enrich our relationship with him whom we love and serve. As he sacrificed for us, we would live sacrificial lives for him. We express our thanks and ask your blessing in his name. Amen.

---

1. W. A. Welsh in *Villains On White Horses*. The Bethany Press, 1964, pp. 43-44. Used by permission.

The Clapping of the Pierced Hands

The Text: I have been crucified with Christ; . . . and the life I now live in the flesh I live by faith in the Son of God, who loved me and gave himself for me.

—Galatians 2:20

Additional Scripture: Romans 8:1-14.

The Meditation: John Henry Jowett was a distinguished English clergyman who profoundly believed that anyone who confessed and took upon himself the name of Christ, just had to be a dedicated humanitarian. It was his abiding conviction that one whose spiritual life "fed upon the bread of God" and drank "the royal wine of heaven," must be captured by a concern for the poor and downtrodden.

One day Dr. Jowett presided over a fund-raising effort on behalf of a new orphanage. An aged friend of mine was present when Jowett invited people in the audience to make their financial subscriptions. Thunderous applause broke forth when a wealthy country squire jumped to his feet immediately to offer a substantial donation. Others followed his example as the hand-clapping showed the gathering's approval of the gifts given.

However, as the contributions to the fund became smaller and smaller, the applause diminished noticeably. And when a poor widow rose to her feet and announced that she would give the maximum she could afford, an English pound which, in those days, was worth about five dollars, silence greeted her offer. Disturbed noticeably by such a rude lack of gratitude, Dr. Jowett stood looking out the window for a long minute, his silence falling like divine judgment over the people. Then, with a touch of emotion, he whispered: "Listen, listen, I think I hear the clapping of the pierced hands!"

When at this Sacramental Table we are subdued by the splendor of Christ's self-giving for us, yielding up our lives to his control, we shall know that his "love so amazing, so divine" demands all we are and have. Those pierced hands of his will applaud such surrender of life to his will and service.

Prayer for the Loaf: O Living Christ, the Word made flesh, grant us as we break this symbol of your broken Body that the life of self-giving, which was in you, may also be in us. With gratitude we pray. Amen.

Prayer for the Cup: Gracious Lord, from the chalice of whose life was poured out the wine of redeeming love, we pray that your Spirit of sacrifice may be in us also. For your sake and ours. Amen.

Frank Edmund See
Minneapolis, Minnesota

Service for Homebound and Hospitalized

The Text: "Blessed are those who hunger and thirst for righteousness, for they shall be satisfied. . . . For where two or three are gathered in my name there am I in the midst of them."

—Matthew 5:6; 18:20

Hymns: (One or more; the following are suggestions): "Blessed Assurance," "I am Thine, O Lord," "In the Cross of Christ I Glory," "Break Thou the Bread of Life."

Additional Scripture: (One or more of the following) Psalm 23, Psalm 46, Isaiah 53:1-12 and 41:10, John 14:1-15, Phillipians 4:4-9.

The Meditation: We may partake of the emblems in confidence and with the assurance that our Lord is here to bless. He has promised that where two or three or more are gathered in his name he is present. We participate in the Lord's Supper at his invitation and in the glorious tradition of his church since the time he said, "This is my body. . . . Do this in remembrance of me" (Luke 22:19-20). In our partaking, we enter into a worldwide fellowship with other Christians, and we have a New Testament precedent for partaking in the home. Members of the early church met in fellowship, prayer, and in the breaking of bread together from "house to house." (See Acts 2:42, 46.)

While we would like to be with other Christians in the House of the Lord, we are assured by the words of Jesus that God is not confined to any certain mountain or temple or church building and that "true worshipers will worship the Father in spirit and truth" (John 4:21-23). And when the conditions of life are beyond our control, we can claim the promise, "I will never fail you nor forsake you" (Hebrews 13:5b). It is our prayer and confidence that as we remember the Lord Jesus in partaking of the emblems, he will sanctify this place by his presence.

Words of Institution: (One of the following passages): Matthew 26:26-28, Mark 14:22-24, Luke 22:14-20, 1 Corinthians 11:23-26. (You will find them printed in the front part of this book.)

Prayer of Blessing: Our Father, who has promised to be "a very present help," we express our thanks for the privilege of partaking of the Lord's Supper. This loaf and this cup are offered in remembrance of and in love for our Savior who gave himself for us. May these emblems be a source of spiritual blessing as they are received in faith, and grant that this act of obedience and worship be a source of added hope and strength. Give a genuine sense of your divine presence and transform the common or monotonous into a holy adventure. We pray with thanksgiving in the name of Jesus who was victorious over both life and death, and to him be our praise. Amen.

Partaking of Emblems: (The emblems may be served by a minister, or an elder; or members of the group may serve one another. When elements ordinarily used in the church are not available, special elements may be prepared in almost any home and consecrated to this holy purpose.)

Prayer of Thanks: We thank you, our Father, for the love expressed and the assurance given. We thank you for this Christian home (or hospital room), and for all who show their love and care. It has been good to share the bread and fruit of the vine in memory of Jesus and in the acknowledgment of his love. May his peace abide. Amen.

Hymn: "Have Thine Own Way, Lord," "Blest Be the Tie that Binds," "The Old Rugged Cross," "When I Survey the Wondrous Cross," (or one chosen by the person or persons served).

Benediction: Read or repeat together a familiar verse such as Psalm 19:14.[1]

---

1. The above service is only suggestive and may be varied to fit the occasion. In the case of a very ill or hospitalized person, the service should be shortened or limited to the words of institution, prayer, and the partaking. The above service may be used many times by varying the songs and scripture and using meditations from other parts of this book.

A Maundy Thursday Service

(Widespread among congregations of The Christian Church (Disciples of Christ), is the celebration of Holy Communion on the evening of the Thursday before Easter, known as Maundy Thursday. Quite often this service is held by candlelight, which adds to the effectiveness and beauty. The room may be entirely lighted by candle or, in addition to the candles, the house lights may be dimmed to give the candleglow effect. In some churches, the youth serve as candle bearers and, in addition to lighting the candles which have been previously placed, they stand in the aisles throughout the service to give light to the worshipers.

It is suggested that this service be conducted somewhat differently from those held on Sunday mornings. This will give an unaccustomed and fresh approach to the observance. In some buildings, a rearrangement of the table, pulpit and other chancel furniture will help to accent the occasion. It is a time for creativity and innovation. If the congregation usually partakes individually as the emblems are passed, it would be well at the Maundy Thursday service to have the members partake simultaneously. In this latter method, each communicant retains the bread and the cup and all partake at the same time as instructed by the person presiding. The service should proceed with as few announcements as possible.

Some congregations dramatize the service by presenting a living picture of the Last Supper. Individuals around the table in such a picture may be in modern dress or that of ancient times. Mark 14:26 tells us that "when they had sung a hymn, they went out." Following the Maundy Thursday candlelight observance of the Lord's Supper, it is effective to have members of the congregation leave row by row while singing the closing hymn. The candles should remain lit until the room is emptied. Offering plates may be placed at the doors for use by those who would like to give for world hunger or other worthy causes. The following service is suggestive. It may be varied by using other material from this book.)

The Night He was Betrayed

The Text: When it was evening, he sat at table with the twelve disciples; and as they were eating, he said, "Truly, I say to you, one of you will betray me." And they were very sorrowful, and began to say to him one after another, "Is it I, Lord?"
—Matthew 26:20-22

Additional Scripture: Mark 14:17-26.

The Call to Commune: "Come to me, all who labor and are heavy-laden, and I will give you rest. Take my yoke upon you, and learn from me; for I am gentle and lowly in heart, and you will find rest for your souls."
—Matthew 11:28-29

Hymn: "Come, Thou Almighty King," or " 'Tis Midnight, and on Olive's Brow."

The Invocation: Gracious God, hallowed be your name forever, we come this evening with humble and expectant hearts to this hour of Holy Communion. Help us to search our own beings under the light of your love, and grant us strength to be true to our commitment which we have made through confession and baptism. In this quiet fellowship, we seek a oneness with one another and with our Master as we break bread together at his Table. In Christ's name, we pray. Amen.

The Meditation: The disciples' question, "Lord, is it I?" echos and re-echos in our minds as we wait before this table upon which are the emblems of our redemption. Probably none of us would betray our Lord in the same way it was done on that tragic night long ago, but in other ways, are we guiltless? It is well for us to follow the apostle Paul's advice, "Let a man examine himself, and so eat of the bread and drink of the cup" (1 Cor. 11:28). It is possible that some of us have tried to serve two masters, or we have compromised our convictions, or have not lived up to the commitment we once made. It may be that some of us have let selfish aims come between us and our Lord. At this table, each of us should ask him to point out those shoddy places in our lives, and to give us a greater determination to live more Christlike.

However, our attention must not dwell upon our unworthiness, it must be focused upon the Christ who is the central figure of any worthy Communion

Service. We look to him for our forgiveness and hear him say, "go in peace" (Luke 8:48). As we spend time at the Lord's Table, we are drawn closer together and into a closer relationship with our Master. With these thoughts in mind on this Maundy Thursday, let us be thankful for all that the emblems represent, including his suffering, death, resurrection, and promise. Let us also remember that through Christ's sacrifice we have redemption and eternal life.

Hymn: "Let Us Break Bread Together." (This may be sung by a soloist, by the choir, or by the entire congregation.)

Prayer for the Loaf: Our Father and our God, we acknowledge that we are here because of your mercy and grace. In the quietness of this evening hour, we would rethink and relive the experience which took place in the upper room so long ago. We hear the Christ say, "Take, eat; this is my body," and we sense both the glory and the tragedy of the occasion. Bless the loaf as we partake, and may your Spirit breathe upon us that we may live in the newness of life made possible for all who are in Christ Jesus. In his name, we pray. Amen.

The Distribution of the Bread: Jesus said, "This is my body which is broken for you. Do this in remembrance of me."

Prayer for the Cup: Gracious and loving Lord, from whom life itself comes, we humbly express our thanks for this cup which speaks so eloquently of the Savior's blood shed for our salvation. Help us tonight in this beautiful service to appropriate its blessings for our soul's health and happiness. It is truly a hallowed experience to participate once again in this feast of remembrance. Bless this cup to our spiritual strengthening and may we go from here tonight with a continuing sense of the divine Presence. This we ask in Jesus' name. Amen.

The Distribution of the Cup: Jesus said, "This is my blood of the covenant, which is poured out for many. Do this in remembrance of me."

Hymn: "I Bind My Heart This Tide," or "They'll Know We Are Christians by Our Love."

Benediction: "Now may the Lord of peace himself give you peace at all times in all ways. The Lord be with you all" (2 Thesselonians 3:16).

Hymn (as the people leave the sanctuary): "Amazing Grace," or "Pass It On."

Communion Poems

Bread

Be gentle
   When you touch bread.
Let it not lie
   Uncared for—unwanted.
So often bread
   Is taken for granted.
There is so much beauty
   In bread—
Beauty of sun and soil,
   Beauty of patient toil.
Winds and rains have caressed it,
   Christ often blessed it.
Be gentle
   When you touch bread.[1]

—*Author Unknown*

---

1. *Quoted in Masterpieces of Religious Verse.* Harper & Row, 1948. Used by permission of Harper & Row.

The Last Supper

*The twelve with Christ reacted when he said
To them that, "One among you shall betray."
They watched Him as He took the sop of bread.
Then "Is it I?" they heard each other say.
And we can see ourselves at times with Him,
For we have traits so much akin to theirs;
A strong resolve, a weakened vow, a whim,
And in our wheat of love, we find the tares.*

*Today as then the question must be asked,
For hearts betray the One who loved them so,
And "Is it I?" may find the sin unmasked,
That He may then again in grace bestow
True love's forgiveness for the likes of me,
And set the soul toward love's eternity.*
—Carlton C. Buck

Past Bread and Wine

*The proffered cup, the broken bread,
The silence of this holy place,
The gleaming white of Table spread,
Are nought—unless my soul embrace
Beyond this ancient rite, outpoured,
The Presence of the Living Lord!*[2]
—Bernice Ayers Hall

---

2. *The Christian Evangelist-Front Rank*, October 4, 1959.

Blest Feast of Love Divine

Blest feast of love divine!
'Tis grace that makes us free
To feed upon this bread and wine,
In mem'ry, Lord, of Thee.

That blood which flowed for sin,
In symbol here we see,
And feel the blessed pledge within,
That we are loved by Thee.

O, if this glimpse of love
Be so divinely sweet,
What will it be, O Lord, above,
Thy gladd'ning smile to meet!

—Sir Edward Denny

Let us Break Bread Together

Let us break bread together
On our knees;
Let us drink wine together
On our knees;
Let us praise God together
On our knees.
When I fall on my knees,
With my face to the rising sun,
O Lord, have mercy on me.

—Spiritual

Draw Us Near to Thee, Dear Lord
(Communion Hymn.[3])

Draw us near to Thee, dear Lord,
Speak to us thy holy Word.
May we lay aside each care
As in fellowship we share.

Break the bread again, dear Lord,
Pour the cup as thou hast poured.
Let us hear the words unsaid,
Bless each cup, each piece of bread.

Grant forgiveness for our sin,
Help us see thy love therein.
Love has paid redemption's price,
Faith accepts thy sacrifice.

Draw us near to Thee, dear Lord,
Speak again thy holy Word.
May our sleeping joys awake
As in faith we now partake.

—Carlton C. Buck

---

3. Lorenz Publishing Company, Dayton, Ohio, owner. Used by permission.

Partaking

Father, I need you—
With the communion cup
Held tight
Against my frailties,
The self in your image
Swells to meet you.
The stained-glass hymns,
The words
Rain down,
Watering
My tomorrows.[4]

—Mary G. Faulconer

Make Ready

Make ready the table.
Make ready the room,
And fill all the vases
With freshly cut bloom.

Make ready the emblems,
The loaf and the juice,
Those once consecrated
For this special use.

Prepare for His Presence.
Make ready each part,
And while you're preparing,
Make ready the heart.

—Carlton C. Buck

---
4. *The Disciple,* May 18, 1975

Bread of Love

Give me, Lord, the bread of life,
broken bread for me,
the bread of love giv'n by Christ,
giv'n on Calvary.

In my hunger and my thirst,
food of love afford,
In my hunger nourish me,
O my God and Lord.

When decisions come to me,
I must choose a way,
Fill my heart with peace and hope;
lead me, Lord, I pray.

That I may the bliss attain,
promised in Thy Word.
Bring me to maturity,
O my God and Lord.[5]

—Dale Miller

---

5. From "Let Us Break Bread Together—a folk Communion Service." Bethany Press, 1971, p. 34. Used by permission.

Come Now to His Table

Come now to His Table,
Come softly in prayer
Meet here with the Saviour,
Communion to share.
Come, break bread together
In light from above;
Eat here of His mercy,
Drink here of His love.

"Take, this is my body,"
Thus saith the Lord;
The wine of redemption
Our Saviour has poured.
"Do this in remembrance,"
His death to proclaim;
Come, meet at His table,
Partake in His name.

The Table of promise
Endowed with His grace.
Aglow with His presence
Make hallowed this place.
Come break bread together
In light from above;
Eat here of His mercy,
Drink here of His love.[6]

—*Carlton C. Buck*

---

6. From Anthem: "Come Now To His Table." Used by permission, Boston Music Co. Boston, Mass., copyright owner.

Communion

"I am the bread of life," the Saviour said,
And with the loaves, and words,
Men are fed;
"I am the vine," God's Son taught,
"My father is the husbandman—ye, branches,
Which he wrought."

"This is my body, broken for thee," the Master said,
While breaking in his hands
The apostles' bread;
"This my blood was shed for thee"—he took the cup,
Bidding his friends take theirs, too, and
With him sup.

O Broken Bread, broken for me, O Living Bread!
O Bruised Vine, bruised for me, Sustaining Vine!
Let me take up the cup—remembering
A hungry world, broken and unfed,
People athirst for thee, adrift, misled,
Needing, as Galileans needed, thee! . . . O living
Vine and Bread![7]

—Mary Dickerson Bangham

---

7. Charles L. Wallis ed., *Worship Resources for the Christian Year.* Harper & Row, 1954, p. 193. Used by permission.

Together We Break Bread

The years have passed, but would it be
  A far cry to assume
The Table there was spread for me
  In that large Upper Room?

No! for He invites those who will,
  "Take, eat" the Master said.
He blessed it then, and blesses still,
  And thus our souls are fed.

Come, join with me, sit at His feet,
  Hear what the Master said.
We fellowship there as we eat,
  Together we break bread.

—*Carlton C. Buck*

Index of Scripture

Exodus	page
3:1-5	81
16:13-36	97
Numbers	
15:37-41	87
Deuteronomy	
8:3	58
1 Chronicles	
29:6-14	64
Psalms	
4:7	92
19:14	136
20:7	87
23	79, 134
23:1-6	79
42:1-2	84
46	134
100:1-5	101
122:1	8, 91
130:1-8	111
Ecclesiastes	
12:1	87
Isaiah	
41:10	134
53:1-6	126
53:1-12	134
55:1b-2a	16
55:6-13	16

Matthew	page
5:1-12	83
5:6	83, 134
10:24-33	128
10:42	128
11:25-30	14
11:28-29	138
14:15-20	24
16:13-24	124
18:20	39, 134
26:19	89
26:20-22	138
26:26-28	58, 135
26:26-30	10, 58
26:36-46	69
28:5-7	39
28:16-20	39
28:19-20	105
28:20b	39

Mark	
12:29-31a	69
14:12-16	89
14:17-26	138
14:22-24	10, 135
14:22-26	93
14:24	47
14:26	138

Luke	
4:14-21	26
4:18	27
8:48	140
9:18-26	37
18:9-14	107
19:1-10	18

	page
22:10-23	12
22:11	77
22:14-19	11
22:14-20	135
22:19-20	87, 93, 134
24:30-31	113

John	
1:14	56
3:16	89
4:7-24	28
4:21-23	135
6:1-14	113
6:25-33	122
6:35	97
6:48	37
6:51	122
10:1-12	22
10:10b-18	50
13:31-38	60
13—17	11
14:1-15	134
14:15	60
14:23	70
15:1-17	103
15:13	55, 82
17:1-11	30
17:21	62

Acts	
1:8	99
2:38-39	99
2:38-47	41
2:41-47	91
2:42	41, 117, 134
2:46	134
17:22-31	105
20:7	41, 46

Romans
1:16-17 99
8:1-14 132
8:26 111

1 Corinthians
1:18-25 130
2:9-16 54
6:19b-20 109
10:14-24 35
10:16 . . . . . 54, 85
10:16-22 85
10:31-33 85
11:2 95
11:18-26 130
11:23-26 . . . . .
. . 11, 31, 41, 119, 135
11:24 . . . . 35, 126
11:24b 26, 116
11:26 . 30, 35, 73, 130
11:27-34 52
11:28 139
11:29 54
12:1-14 62
15:20-28 73

2 Corinthians
4:1-6 45
4:15 64
5:19 95
8:1-9 115
9:15 70
12:7-10 48
12:9 48

Galatians
2:20 132
6:1-10 32
6:14 32

Ephesians
2:13 21
2:18-20 20
2:19b 67
3:1-12 56
3:14-20 20
4:1-8 67

Philippians
4:4-9 134

Colossians
1:9-18 71

2 Thessalonians
3:16 141

1 Timothy
3:1-3 9

2 Timothy
2:8-19 . . . . . 75, 87

Titus
1:7-9 9

Hebrews
11:1-5 95
8:6-13 119
13:5b 135

1 Peter
1:13-21 109

1 John
1:1-10 117
1:7 . . . . . 95, 117
4:19 54
5:1-12 43

Revelation
3:20-22 77
21:5 18

Topical Index

	page
Act of Faith, An	95
Bread and Wine and Money	64
Bread for the World	97
Breaking Bread Together	58
Breaking the Loaves With the Hungry	24
Broken for You	126
Called to Be Wholly Present	81
Carefully and Prayerfully Prepared	89
Clapping of the Pierced Hands, The	132
Communion: A Blessing in Any Language	105
Communion and Its Underlying Purpose	35
Community of Faith, A	20
Discerning His Body	54
Don't Forget Me	26
Entrance into His Presence	14
Essential To a Life of Faith	16
Expanding Our Capacities	50
For a Hungry World	122
For the Redemption of Mankind	30
Fresh Revelatory Encounter, A	41
Gladness in His Presence	91
God Hears Our Silence	111
God Reveals Himself	45
Grace Transforms Weakness into Power	48
Guest Room, The	77
Here Is Offered Renewal	32
His Grace at Work in Us	52
His Gracious Invitation	37
I Have Called You Friends	103
Let God Speak to Us	101
Let's Go to Jerusalem	12
Let Us Celebrate Our New Life	22

Look For the Cross and Find the Church	124
Lord's Supper Is for All People, The	107
Love Seeks and Thirsts	83
Love: The First Commandment	69
Man's Rememberer	93
Maundy Thursday Service, A	137
Meal of Many Themes	117
Meal of Memory, The	75
Miracle of Bread, The	113
Moments of Sacred Fellowship	43
New Covenant to God's People, A	119
Our Common Faith	67
Preeminence of Christ, The	71
Proclaiming the Lord's Death	130
Re-Creative Work of God, The	18
Sacred Appointment, A	46
Service for the Homebound & Hospitalized	134
So You Shall Remember	87
Table Before Me, A	79
Table of Grace, The	115
This Cup Called Life	128
Time to Remember and Obey	60
Ultimate Need of Mankind, The	73
Unseen Host at Every Meal, The	39
We Belong to God	109
We Celebrate Our Oneness	62
We Come As Needy Persons	28
We Follow Jesus' Admonition	85
Witnessing for Christ Today	99
Word Became Flesh, The	56

Index of Authors

	page
Barnes, Carnella J.	119
Betzer, Frank L.	45
Bingham, Walter D.	22
Blair, James L.	32
Bowers, Vernon H.	37
Carnes, J. Sydney	73
Christensen, James L.	93
Davis, Herbert P.	101
Elliott, Dulcina B.	20
Evans, Fredrick Ross	124
Evans, Lorenzo J.	30
Feltner, Faye	97
Ferrer, Luis E.	105
Gaylord, Raymond	107
Haggard, Forest D.	56
Havens, Jasper C.	89
Henry, Enoch W., Jr.	26
Howland, William C., Jr.	81
Hylton, Samuel W.	18
Joyce, J. Daniel	16
Lowrey, Sadie	28
MacGowan, Walter F.	69
Merrick, Daniel B.	77
Miller, Mary Lou	24
Moak, James A.	48
Naff, Jack	52
Overton, Patrick	111
Read, Gordon A.	115
Rousseau, Tom	128
See, Frank Edmund	132
Teegarden, Kenneth L.	41
Watkins, Keith	64
Welch, Rosa Page	85
Wheeler, J. Clyde	12
Woolfolk, Jean	60

Index of Poems

Blest Feast of Love Divine—Sir Edward Denny	144
Bread—Anon	142
Bread of Love—Dale Miller	147
Come Now to His Table—Carlton C. Buck	148
Communion—Mary Dickerson Bangham	149
Draw Us Near to Thee, Dear Lord—Carlton C. Buck	145
In Sweet Communion—John Newton	4
Let Us Break Bread Together—Spiritual	144
Make Ready—Carlton C. Buck	146
Partaking—Mary G. Faulconer	146
Past Bread and Wine—Bernice Ayers Hall	143
The Last Supper—Carlton C. Buck	143
Together We Break Bread—Carlton C. Buck	150